A NEW EDUCATION FOR
NEW MINDS

A Conversation about
Mind-Centered Learning

Marquis R. Nave

A NEW EDUCATION FOR NEW MINDS
A CONVERSATION ABOUT MIND-CENTERED LEARNING

iUniverse books may be ordered through booksellers or by contacting:

iUniverse LLC
1663 Liberty Drive
Bloomington, IN 47403
www.iuniverse.com
1-800-Authors (1-800-288-4677)

ISBN: 978-1-4917-4101-6 (sc)
ISBN: 978-1-4917-4100-9 (hc)
ISBN: 978-1-4917-4099-6 (e)

Library of Congress Control Number: 2014913010

Printed in the United States of America.

iUniverse rev. date: 08/04/2014

I
am
that which I
have forgotten

What is the highest potential of our minds? How can education help answer this question?

Contents

Part I: Keys to a New Mind and a New Education

Preface: Ideas of Me 1

Introduction 8

1. Beyond Words, There Is Knowledge 17

2. Perception versus Knowledge 24

3. The New Education: Mind-Centered Learning 32

4. Definition of a True Teacher 40

5. A Student Is Not the Same as an Attendee 46

6. A Mind-Centered Education: Ego, Time, and Money 51

Part II: Keys to a System of Writing

7. The Goal of Writing Is To... 61

8. The Supremacy of Sentence Structure 68

9. The God of the Essay 76

10. Grammar Plain and Simple 121

Sacred Scrolls and Scripts
(Thank Yous and Dedications)

This book is my dedication to education. I owe this book to education. Anyone who knows me knows that education is my passion. As a matter of fact this book helped me realize that education was my gateway drug to knowledge. Education served as a mental high for me. It hooked me like the cold warmth of heroine, the surreal buzz of marijuana, the dislocation of alcohol, the euphoria of cocaine, or the numbing effect of painkillers. From the sacred hallways and the holy classrooms to the rigid registration centers, I give to you my best thinking—an offering of another way to perceive education, learning, and knowledge. In my classrooms I have seen brilliance shine from various minds, and I have read the work of many brilliant minds whom I have never personally met. I have devoted myself for the last ten years to understanding the mind. That research, study, and practice have been put together in these pages, in the most coherent way I know how, for the purposes of starting a serious conversation on a new educational paradigm.

I am thankful to Fullerton College for hiring me straight out of my degree program. Philip Mayfield, Mark Knoernschild, Constance Eggers, Miguel Powers, and Tamara Trujillo made positive personal impressions in my teaching and experience at that school. To the stars who graced me with their presence for a semester or two, thank you for letting me teach you, and thank you for teaching me. To those who offered their work as examples for this book, thank you. To one student in particular, Tyler Garcia, who did research work for me and added his brilliance to this book, thank you. And to the Cerritos College family, who created an atmosphere that made me feel welcomed enough to bring my kids around, thank you for the freedom and encouragement to chart my own course. Linda Rose, Jack Swanson, and Megalis Lopez were very helpful to me and made me feel welcomed. To the many creative minds and brave souls who endured my classes, thank you. You guys inspired me because you worked hard not only to stick it out for an entire semester but also to expand your minds.

Part I

Keys to a New Mind and a New Education

I think they want the idea of me rather than the true me!
—Me

Preface: Ideas of Me

In the summer of 1995, when I took the placement test before my first year of community college, I placed in the lowest, most remedial classes Long Beach City College had to offer. The placement test scores confirmed a deep, abiding suspicion that had built up over my thirteen years of being educated. Yep, I was officially dumb. That test was the confirmation of my stupidity, a very visual, mathematically quantifiable report of it. A part of me felt immersed in shameful ignorance, and another part of me felt angry. I was genuinely shocked that I had gone through thirteen-plus years of being "educated" but still knew so little. I had graduated, although not on time, from high school and received my high school diploma. That was supposed to mean that I was able to meet minimum academic standards. And although I hadn't put much effort into my education, I'd still thought that my high school education would have prepared me better. To have my ignorance officially confirmed like that made me feel as if I had been under some kind of delusion, a delusion of grandeur. It was as if I was being forced out of a self-deluded state that had been engrained and conditioned in me throughout the years of my stint in the American educational system.

I had failed to meet the minimum standards of the local community college. Where was my education? It was evident from my placement test scores that I had not learned much. The truth is that in high school I had thought education had very little value, so I put very little effort into studying and learning. I believed that education would magically happen to me if I just simply showed up to class. No effort was actually required on my part. High school seemed to me to be about memorization, regurgitation, and test performance rather than learning. I passed high school, and I got my diploma—but I did not *learn* anything. I was trained to do work, not to learn or think.

I was eighteen when I began my first year of college. Long Beach City College had the best football team in the area, and that was my reason for going there. I was the typical pompous, conceited football jock. I sincerely expected that after high school I would go play at a big-name Division I college. It was a shock to my mind that I was not given the golden ticket of a football scholarship. Instead, I had a tragic football story, one I will avoid telling here. And I was absolutely unprepared for the reality of the deterioration of my Division I dreams. I was a simple, untrained, underemployed, uneducated man-boy. My world twirled about in dizzying chaos, night and day. I had no idea what to expect out of my life. My life seemed to diminish to a droning lifeless passage of time. I felt lost in an ocean of pity, anger, judgment, and self-doubt with no point of origin and no land in sight. The world very quickly became to me a threatening, menacing place with mal intent.

In response to my perceptions, I became mean, cynical, and bitter. I walked around the Long Beach City College campus feeling angry, afraid, insecure, and hopeless. I no longer knew who I was without the identity, status, and security that football had offered me all those years. I had believed that football was going to carry me through life; it had been my source of self-esteem and self-worth. After I could no longer identify myself as a football player, I found myself in identity no-man's land. I wasn't a student, and I was no longer an athlete. Working at least two jobs, attending school full-time, and giving up on playing football was taking its toll on my frail state of mind. My life was dramatically shifting in a direction I expended a lot of energy trying to resist. It really seemed to me as if some evil force had vengefully snatched from my clinched fist that last tenuous strand of hope.

One day after my third semester at City College, my best friend, Mike Glenn, approached me in our small one-bedroom apartment in Long Beach. In a solemn voice, he told me that he could no longer respect me because he knew that I was simply cheating myself out of an opportunity to be better. Mike, short and stocky, with almost translucent skin, looked at me with such compassion that his short, stocky, and translucent self disappeared. It was like some infinite part of him was speaking to some infinite part of me. His face was warm and nervous, a sure sign of sincerity. His challenge pushed me toward the precipice of a major life decision—one that would cause me to make a foundational shift in my perception. His inquisition was really like a higher order from something within me, like being called to while in a deep, deep sleep, one that I never really want to wake up from. My friend could see past the dull shine I had offered the world and see the brilliant potential that was beyond even my own awareness at the time. He simply held up a mirror to show me a better me.

I had no clue if I could actually do any better than I was already doing. By that time, three semesters in, I had quit playing football and had completed fewer than 15 units that were transferable to a Cal State University. The fumes of victimhood were beginning to overwhelm me. Mike's challenge helped spur me toward a higher me and somehow distract me from a lesser me. That interaction, which was a true moment of inspiration, sparked something within me. He was my teacher in that moment. And had he only come into my life for that one occasion, I would be eternally grateful. This book really began on that day!

I took his challenge very seriously. I also wanted to prove to myself that I could do better. So I started to ask questions of people who seemed like good students: how to take notes, what they did to study better, and so on. I talked to my teachers before and after class when I didn't understand something. I studied and read all the material until I felt I had a reasonable understanding of it. I read carefully and annotated my readings. I looked up words I did not understand. I used my spare time to study and get extra help in whatever area I was having trouble.

In other words, I applied myself. I earned a 3.75 GPA and established my academic mojo that first semester after I took my friend's challenge. I never looked back after that. I lusted after As and despised Bs, which are a graduate's version of Fs. In the end, I earned my B.A. in English with an emphasis in creative writing and later went on to earn my M.F.A in creative writing, both from Cal State University of Long Beach. I proved to myself that my intelligence was very capable of satisfying academia's standards. I gained confidence and overall academic skill. But this was not the true victory; academia was only a proving ground. This period also (unbeknownst to me at the time) ignited a search for my higher potential.

I fell into teaching English at the community college level. Very shortly into my teaching career, though, I struck gold. What I call "the great insight" came to me after I asked a primarily young, vibrant group of students at one of my colleges to respond to an in-class essay prompt that basically presented them with this question: "Why does it seem that students are afraid to think critically?" These three responses came up most often: (1) We are afraid of being viewed as stupid. (2) We have rarely been asked or required to think. (3) We don't have confidence in the quality of our thoughts. Those answers revealed to me the role that mind has played in constructing those students' ability to learn and their ability to think creatively. Their beliefs and perceptions about their mental capabilities have one of two effects: (1) they impose limitations on the creative force or (2) they liberate the creative force. Mind in this book is defined as the nonphysical activating agent for creative thought; thought is mind's activating mechanism. Focused thought, then, can be likened to an intensifier of creative thinking. Limiting beliefs about one's own mental capabilities have a power that can hold that creative force in a mental quarantine. I came to realize that freeing this creative force is the goal of teaching and education.

In the 1960's, Ivy League professors Richard Alpert and Timothy Leary used the effect of drugs, in particular psilocybin, on the mind to study human consciousness. Mind-altering drugs are an attempt to access this creative spark within our minds. I am not endorsing drug use. I am simply pointing out that there is a strong desire within humans to access that creative function of mind. Respected artists from every genre will readily admit to this. And this desire for mental liberation even spawned a generation that had the greatest impact on American society. However, creative thinking is not about coming up with an interesting expressive way to communicate. Creative thinking as defined in this book is the ability to reach into knowledge or into a broader awareness in order to bring forth new informative ideas that help humanity evolve or realize greater power within each individual. Knowledge is defined as the potential that exist in creative thought. From this generation, more creative thinking will enter the world. Actually, the expression of creative thought is the blessing of this generation. Professor Gerard Puccio, author of *The Creative Thinker's Toolkit* (2014), makes it clear that creative thinking is a skill that we can develop. Thinking that is genuinely creative comes from knowledge, which begins the process of developing a new mind.

Education, then, is a process of realizing one's creative potential. Therefore, their academic performance must be measured differently because limitations in the mind are *the* definitive factor regarding their academic performance. This new understanding helped me realize that teaching was an opportunity to meet individuals on a mental plane. I was being introduced to their minds, and they were being introduced to mine. This is why the mind is the center of education. This also made me see that I must aim my teaching at the mind, not the brain. But I knew next to nothing of the mental plane. So I went on a journey to understand how this mental plane functions. I am not talking about psychology but a plane of mind. This mental plane or mind has a set of laws that do not correspond to physical laws, for instance, quantum entanglement: a physical phenomenon that occurs when pairs or groups of particles are generated or interact in ways such that the quantum state of each particle *cannot be described independently*—instead, a quantum state may be given for the system as a whole. Our physics can't explain *why* this is. But understanding the mind can help us understand phenomenon like quantum entanglement because the mental plane's first law is wholeness.

A new education must seriously consider the mind's role in all that pertains to learning, knowledge, and bettering this world. A new education is built on the idea that the mind is purely creative and there nothing outside the mind; this is an idea I share with George Berkeley. All that is perceivable is mind made. All that is imperceptible to the body's senses becomes temporarily unknowable to the mind because the mind has been conditioned to "know" only according to sensory data or through concepts. This is why knowledge involves a process of extending beyond one's personal awareness into the broader awareness. This is the new education being presented here. It is possible for the mind to reach into a reservoir of pure creative space through direct realization. What philosophy and education and society at large are asking is this one question: Does your knowledge help me?

A new mind no longer mistakes processing for learning or perception for knowledge. A new mind is in the midst of realizing its creative powers. Perception is limited. Knowledge is unlimited. Processing fosters "learning" at the perceptual level. Knowledge involves direct realization; therefore, perception is not involved at all. Knowledge produces creative thinking, and creative thinking changes our perception. It is truly a process. For conversation's sake, consider this: What if our education system can help produce minds that are constantly connected to creative thought? *A New Education for New Minds* claims that creating is the highest function of the mind, and this is because the mind is really a creator, not a learner. But until the mind realizes this, there is need for learning. And it is this learning that comes from a new education. New minds can help create a curriculum that will build a new educational system. We must begin to attempt to learn everything we can about the mind because the mind is the center of learning.

Few are those who see with their own eyes
and feel with their own hearts.

. . .

Education is what remains after one has forgotten
what one has learned in school.

. . .

A man should look for what is, and not for what he thinks should be.
—Albert Einstein

Introduction

"The first illusion, which must be displaced before another thought system can take hold, is that it is a sacrifice to give up the things of this world. . . . It is the idea of sacrifice that makes him blind" (Schucman 1976). The world comes to us as it appears according to our perceptions. I know Ayn Rand is rolling over in her grave regarding the ideas in this book. Well, I would be honored if she even batted a ghostly eye, really. *A New Education for New Minds* was born from my quest to know what learning, education, and knowledge actually mean. And how does the mind relate to all of these? What I realized is that every single one of these inquiries involves the mind. What happens when we are being educated? How do we define learning? What is knowledge? For educators, the mission to raise the bar of education in this country starts with these questions. These questions require new perspectives, new ways of looking at the same old thing. And that is why a new education is based on learning that results from shifting one's perspective and eventually moving from perception to knowledge, from brain-centered learning to mind-centered learning.

In Part I of *A New Education for New Minds*, mind-centered learning results from knowledge which comes from a direct realization of a broader awareness that fosters creative thinking. It is beyond perception, far removed from the conceptual realm. Knowledge is in the realm of direct realization. Knowledge comes from a process of extending beyond one's personal awareness to a broader awareness. In this broader awareness is creative thought. The goal of the new educational model is to help students experience this shift—from the personal awareness to the broader awareness, or from perception to knowledge. Before this fundamental shift, we go from misperception to misperception. This jumping from illusion to illusion is an insane attempt to make what is illusory in nature into something permanent. Once we truly exhaust ourselves with the impossible task of trying to make illusion into truth, we gain the stability required for true perception. One could be said to perceive more truly if one's thinking is without error or untruth. Misperception brings error to the mind, but true perception fosters truth in it. Although neither kind of perception can perceive truth, true perception is the basis for knowing truth. Error and truth are direct opposites with no overlap, just as perception and knowledge are equally, diametrically opposed. Knowing what is true can only be directly realized. Direct realization is the basis for mind-centered learning. The fruits of mind-centered learning are new minds that are wholly creative.

From a Western scientific point of view, it is hard to accept that the mind exists without the brain. From a scientific materialist perspective, anything that is real must show empirical evidence. This results in the belief that without the brain, there is no mind. But the mind's evidence is so obvious that we can't see it. It is like Poe's story "The Purloined Letter." The evidence of mind is hidden in the obvious. Its proof is our very creative existence, bless Rene Descartes' and Kant's beautiful minds. From Aristotle to Hume to Spinoza, Berkeley and Hegel, the mind has real significance in understanding the world and our experience of it. These philosophers went head to head with the great questions regarding the mind, and all of them produced important ideas that evolved us as a human species. There are ideas that these men expounded upon that I agree with and some that I don't. I have my own ideas concerning the mind; many of which are presented in this book.

For the purposes of our conversation, the mind and the brain are two interrelated yet distinct entities that serve two very different functions. *Origins of the Human Mind* (2013), taught by Professor Stephen P. Hinshaw, an award-winning teacher and clinical psychologist, offers scientific and academic insight into this very topic. The brain does not learn; it carries out the function of processing light and facilitating chemical reactions. Because of its physical structure, the brain has limits to its function. One does not learn because he or she processes information, no more than a computer learns. One learns from attaching meaning to the sensory information that is being processed. What the brain can never do is provide subjective meaning because meaning comes from the ability to observe from another vantage point or perspective. Only the mind can have a perspective. For most people, that perspective is made from the collected data of the various sense organs. But processing is not learning. Processing is a conscious action. But this mode of awareness limits our minds to only perceptual knowledge.

I know this is asking a lot, but I truly believe that the results of this inquiry will light the passageways in the incredibly dark tunnel of education in this country. And all the accompanying politics aside, the bright light is the new mind. This new mind will help the world in ways that are incomprehensible to us now. This new mind is beyond theory yet has practical application to all fields. This kind of education far exceeds the status quo of tests and evaluations and rote learning and regurgitation. It will take a momentous effort by the most creative new minds to make a curriculum that could help build a foundation for a new education. Like academic zombies, many students crave substantive knowledge. Many of them have a thirst for ideas that go beyond the quotidian clichés of education. *A New Education for New Minds* points out that the mind is the source of learning and that knowledge activates creative thought in the mind. And this is the goal of the new education.

In chapter 1, "Beyond Words, There is Knowledge," readers are asked to see what happens in the mind when they withdraw meaning from words, ideas, and symbols. From this new perspective, words only have meaning if there is an agreement between two or more people (or an agreement within one's own mind) about the meaning and value of particular symbols. Here words and their meaning become only tools for communication, not knowledge. *The Four Agreements (1997)* by Don Miguel Ruiz is an eloquent overview of four predominant mental agreements that limit our ability to go beyond our personal awareness. Meaning and value are variables; they fluctuate with the current of our minds. Fluctuations in that current are the changing of meaning and value. The current itself is thought. Meaning and value in the mind are created through the reconciliation of two seemingly opposite thoughts, ideas, or symbols. The agreement achieved through dualistic reasoning is what passes for learning in our current educational system. At best, our current education is producing an education dependent on a representation of a truer world. In this system there is no meaning or value until there is agreement within or without oneself. So we agree and—*poof!*—our world is made. But beyond these representations, deep within the mind is knowledge itself. The creative element of life is within the mind.

Chapter 2, "Perception versus Knowledge," discusses how we neglect real learning and opt for interpretation that requires a limited perspective. Perception and knowledge are fundamentally different. Perception is a human necessity, an interpretation of information. Its necessity lies within its usefulness in human communication and survival. In this context, the function of our mind is to *make* something we can all share and perceive together. *The Spiritual Brain: Science and Religious Experience* (2013) by professor Dr. Andrew Newberg is an excellent course in the scientific investigation of neurotheology, which attempts to explain religious experience and behavior in neuroscientific terms. No matter the beliefs (theistic, pantheistic, or naturalistic) those beliefs pose as our realities, our truths, and our gods. The beliefs can take the form of capitalistic, humanistic, spiritualistic, or scientific ideas. It doesn't matter. Each of these worldviews is organized by beliefs. But the highest function of mind is not to waste its energy weaving narratives for a belief system. No, its supreme function is to express its creative abilities. Perception is limited to the conceptual realm and offers only an interpretation derived from the body's senses. Knowledge offers unlimited creative thought. So we have settled for perception over knowledge, for the law of averages over creative genius.

Chapter 3, "The New Education: Mind-Centered Learning," claims that the new educational system's overall goal is to advance the art and science of returning the mind to its creative function of accessing knowledge. If it is not doing that, it is not education but training. The difference is important. Education results in real mental cultivation. Training results in knowing how to do something. In whatever we study, the material being inconsequential, education should be leading students toward the mastery of their mental activities and facilitating the use of mind for creative thinking. This kind of education will benefit every field in tremendous, unexpected ways. Chapters 4 and 5 turn the discussion toward the key components of the new educational system. We look at how education can develop a way to access knowledge and redefine the purpose for the roles of students and teachers. We are struggling in our education system because we have not evolved our perspective on its purpose and function.

Chapter 4, "Definition of a True Teacher," is self-explanatory. The premise presented in this chapter reframes the role of a teacher from being a tool of training to being a facilitator of mental cultivation. Basically, teachers facilitate students' accessing real knowledge. A true teacher can guide students along the path in a way that shortens their normal learning time. Teachers can use a whisper or a roar, but either way students are learning to access the creative source of their minds. Educators must inspire students to focus their attention inward, to affect the content and direction of their thoughts, and to show them how to access new information. Yes, we must train students in particular methods and skills. Overall, though, we facilitate them in finding answers on their own, within their minds, but outside their personal awareness. When a teacher can demonstrate this with his or her students, that person deserves the title of teacher.

Chapter 5, "A Student Is Not the Same as an Attendee," distinguishes a qualified student from someone who has just paid registration fees to take a class. The word *student* is a title that must be earned. In the same way a teacher demonstrates her ability, the student must prove himself or herself as well. A student who can go beyond personal awareness and show command of creative thinking can be called a student. If a student can demonstrate what was taught, that student is well trained. When students feel inspired, it's the result of something within them that has been sparked through a shift in perspective they had while learning from a true teacher. The role of a student must be distinguished and set aside for those who truly fulfill its function. The title "student" is a unique role that has lost its meaning in the current system of education.

The ideas discussed in chapter 6, "A Mind-Centered Education: Ego, Time, and Money," are central to the purpose of education. This chapter demonstrates how three specific ideas actually chain us to a brain-based learning system. A Mind-Centered Education, takes readers behind what I believe are, for some of us Westerners, the three primary veils that keep the mind from being able to access the new information outside of personal awareness. The average everyday thought cycle is primarily dominated by the ideas of ego (individual perception), time, and money. Ego is a thought system that limits us to a personal perspective. This thought system perpetuates the desire to invest in one's perceptions precisely because the ego made them. The ego is the ultimate human symbol.

Everyone has an idea about whom or what they are. The ego, which identifies itself with the body, needs time and space to exist as separate from other egos. Time and space allow the ego to see itself as the body which is born, ages, and then dies. This mental identification with birth, aging, and dying creates the necessary experience of being limited to a physical body. Most humans are so enchanted by the idea of their ego-made self that it generates the sense of personal importance, the desired livelihood, and the level of comfort. This is what makes money or financial means so important. In large part, for us in the West, our egos rest on our financial well-being. Money, undoubtedly, demands a great chunk of our attention and energy. The ideas of ego, time, and money act like a black hole that sucks our creative abilities into itself. All three "realities" (ego, time, and money) are concepts, temporary stories that we believe to be true. The attempt to make something unreal seem real is the immutable nature of all insanity. In the blink of an eye, all three realities could vanish based on value and meaning. Our personal realities are always changing, and that is because our realities are based on perception not knowledge.

Part II, "Keys to a Science of Writing," introduces a system of writing that offers instructions and methods college students can use to write clearer and more effective essays that satisfy the expectations at this level. Writing well is a clear demonstration of critical and creative thinking. The ability to write well structured, well organized essays expresses the ability to organize and structure thoughts and ideas. These chapters are designed to assist educators in preparing students to learn a particular series of lectures on writing essays. The chapters are presented as a basic system of writing that can be adapted and used to build more complex essays that cultivate minds. Chapter 7, "The Goal of Writing Is to . . .," explains the objective of being able to write at a collegiate level. It offers students some simple but central principles and a few important core skills that students need to demonstrate in order to gain command of their writing. Chapter 8, "The Supremacy of Sentence Structure," makes the case that it is imperative for students to gain command of writing each of the four basic sentence structures (simple, compound, complex, and compound-complex) for college writing. Sentences are vehicles for one's ideas. I also break down the basics of each part of a sentence—the phrase, the dependent clause, and the independent clause—and explain the rules that guide them. Chapter 9, "The God of the Essay," devotes special attention to the definitions of an essay and a thesis claim, the organization of a well-structured, organized essay, and the building of strong paragraphs. I claim that the thesis is the god of an essay. Without a thesis claim, one cannot write an essay. This chapter also discusses the difference between a thesis claim and a thesis statement and takes students through the process of creating essays born from their own thinking. "Grammar Plain and Simple," chapter 10, presents the eight parts of speech in a simple and clear fashion so that students may understand grammar usage and sharpen their grammar skills. It provides definitions, functions, rules, and examples for each of the eight parts of speech, with an explanation of verbals added in.

*The potential to form narratives lies at the upper end of the
scale that measures subjects' ability to function reflectively.
High scores in reflective functioning, in other words, mean that
individuals can elaborate coherent, substantive narratives that
demonstrate metacognitive awareness of how and why they think
a certain way, and what might limit or interfere with gaining
a generally accurate understanding of their own and others'
conscious and unconscious thoughts, intentions, and affects.*
—Esther Rashkin

Chapter 1
Beyond Words, There Is Knowledge

Imagine having a spell cast over you that prevents you from telling
the difference between reality and illusion. Imagine that feeling of
dreaming. In this dream, you are special and unique because you are
the center of the universe and you have some control in how the dream
plays out. The enchantment is very intoxicating because it gives you an
incredible sense of freedom and power. At times the dream turns into
a nightmare, especially when you feel as if things are out of control.
But not even the occasional nightmare is enough to wake you up.

Such a spell would be powerful indeed.

Well, if such a spell existed, words, symbols, beliefs, and
perceptions would be the primary ingredients of this potent potion.
In this world, learning is sacrificed for wishes. Illusions stand in for
reality. This is the world created by perceptions. Perception is reality
as we wish it to be but not as it is, and this becomes our narrative.

When Einstein said that "a man should look for what is, and not for what he thinks should be," he was speaking to the potency of the spell of illusion, the world of words. Our narrative is but a dream made from a world of our own making.

Beyond the words or symbols or representations is knowledge, a state of certainty and creativity. Certainty comes from knowledge because knowledge is constant and unchangeable. Creative thinking is a natural consequence of knowledge. On the other hand, perceiving involves the shifting and changing of reality. We are either perceiving or knowing, but never both at the same time. Perceptions are born of the body's senses. When we perceive, a story is conjured up. The offspring of perception and narrative is the basis of this human reality. So first comes experiences, and then perceptions stabilize. As perceptions stabilize, the stories turn into beliefs that grow into fairytales, horror stories, and happy endings. The human veil of narrative is intricate and multiplicitous. These self-made narratives establish beliefs that are mistaken for knowledge. In this reality, these beliefs restrict our awareness to only what we process through our central nervous systems. Our material reality is a narrative, a fantastical drama of light and vibration and the sensory aftershocks. In this world, the mind is dreaming of interacting with matter, and then our ego provides the story to make the dream seem real. There are stories that are dramatic, others are comic, and some are tragic.

It would be like accidently walking in on a stage play being performed and having no idea that the props and the people arguing or laughing on stage are acting out a scene for a play. Nor do they know. In the same way, we react to our mind-made stories because we have no idea what is real or illusion. This confusion in the mind can only persist if the mind cannot break its addiction to the story. Projecting our story onto the actions we witness is a habit more addictive than any drug, even more addictive than sugar. To feel the truth of this addiction, just try to witness actions without ascribing any meaning to those actions. This is challenging because we are psychologically addicted to meaning, familiarity and consistency. In order to access a broader awareness, we must go beyond words, beyond our self-made narratives. How many times have we believed something to be true and then had our reality change right before our eyes? Remember, realities that change are based on perception, an ever-changing illusion. The physical world is a reality that can be changed by the ideas that come from our minds. It is this truth that is the seed of the new education.

From the viewpoint of the new education, all material matter has an interdependent relationship with our mind. This is the same as the Buddhist notion of "dependent arising": basically, all phenomena are arising together in a mutually interdependent web of cause and effect. In a letter from Einstein to the 1933 Nobel Prize–winning Austrian physicist Erwin Schrödinger, he wrote, "You are the only contemporary physicist . . . who sees that one cannot get around the assumption of reality, if only one is honest. Most of them simply do not see what sort of risky game they are playing with reality—reality as something independent of what is experimentally established" (Barrett 1999). The association of our minds and how they participate in assembling our reality is unmistaken. In his book *Understanding the Secrets of Human Perception*, Peter M. Vishton explains in detail how our perceptual world is constructed. The relationship of mind and matter is unequivocal. How that relationship works is a mystery we must examine. In this book, I make the claim that our minds are making narratives which encompass and co-opt physical matter. This narrative is what we experience as reality. But beyond this mental projection is knowledge.

Just as the brain's function is to interpret sensory patterns from the various senses, the mind has the functions of learning and creating. The brain and mind have a beneficial relationship, yet the mind does not dissipate or diminish due to any physical injury; the mind's *expression* may be hindered but not its *ability*. According to Kara Rogers, biomedical sciences editor for Encyclopedia Britannica, who holds a PhD in pharmacology and toxicology from the University of Arizona,

> It would also be naive to suppose that a function is represented in a particular brain area just because it is disrupted after damage to that area. For example, a tennis champion does not play well with a broken ankle, but this would not lead one to conclude that the ankle is the centre in which athletic skill resides. Reasonably certain conclusions about brain-behavior relationships, therefore, can be drawn only if similar well-defined changes occur reliably in a substantial number of patients suffering from similar lesions or disease states. (*2011*)

Our brains are marvelous devices that our minds use to most easily expresses themselves, but our minds do not wax or wane according to brain function. The expression of our minds may be inhibited or altered, but the mind never loses its creative function. That is why the mind becomes the frontier of learning. And what the mind can learn to do is rewire the brain's neural network.

One of the greatest discoveries of our time is the fact that our neural pathways are malleable and that we can rewire them. Neuroscientists tell us that our neural networks can be relocated by our own mental activity. We can literally change the way our brains are wired. In his book *The Malleable Brain: Benefits and Harm from Plasticity of the Brain,* Dr. Aage R. Moller, a well-respected neuroscience researcher, writes, "The brain does not change its shape in the way formable material can, but it can change the way it functions and how its cells are connected to each other ('wired'). The Activation of neural plasticity can change the way different parts of the brain are connected to each other" (2009). We are at a point in our history where research shows that we can influence brain and central nervous function to a certain degree with our *thoughts*. Again Dr. Moller allows us another peek behind the curtain of narrative:

> Neural plasticity is based on synapses' ability to change the way they work (their efficacy or strength) and it may involve formation or elimination of synapses, nerve fibers and dendrites. Plastic changes also include sprouting and branching of nerve fibers, whereby new connections are created between nerve cells. Death of entire nerve cells (programmed cell deaths, PCD) may occur when neural plasticity is *turned on* [emphasis mine]. It may also cause changes in protein synthesis in nerve cells. Neural plasticity, when turned on, can cause reorganization or remodeling (re-wiring) of parts of the nervous system. (2009)

This research gives us enough reason to infer that our minds are working outside our brains precisely because the change is initiated from our thoughts. This mentation, "when turned on," has the ability to influence our central nervous systems. Dr. Moller uncovers another mental phenomenon:

> Neural plasticity has many similarities with memory but there are also differences. Both memory and

plasticity are based on changes in the brain that occur because of *experience and practice* [emphasis mine]. What has been *learned by practice has to be retrieved actively and voluntarily* [emphasis mine]. However, changes in skills acquired through activation of neural plasticity *by training* [emphasis mine] are there automatically every time the skills are used. (2009)

I believe neuroscience is systematizing the mechanics of the practice of what ancient scientists/philosophers observed as universal or metaphysical laws, like those coming out of Egypt, Greece, India and China. Both modern science and ancient knowledge travel along a single continuum in opposite directions, one *through* our physical technologies (bodily senses especially) and the other beyond the bodily senses, what I call direct realization learning. No matter what route one chooses, both inquiries begin and end with the human mind and all that we identify as being part of the human experience.

In review, a new education facilitates the student in discerning illusion from truth in his own mind. Here, the mind is trained to look beyond the concocted narratives it has accepted from society. And from this new perspective, they have the opportunity to access the broader awareness in order to receive new information. As we move from perception to knowledge, our learning moves from concept to direct realization. If one knows conceptually, one cannot also know *directly*. Direct realization is the way for a student to break the circle of reasoning that comes from perceptual learning. When a student experiences the effect of creative thought, their minds will irrevocably expand. This is the new education for the new mind. When we understand that only the mind learns, ripe minds will being to manifest all over education and they will able to continually access creative thinking. The confidence that students gain from this experience will have immeasurable effects on education and the world at large. As true inspired thinking is experienced enough times, the creative spark is lit within a student. And that student will know the difference between perception and knowledge, illusion and truth. If we can begin to understand that knowledge cannot be found in concepts, we will begin to truly learn. True perception begins from this fundamental discernment.

Discussion Questions:

1. How does the quote at the beginning of the chapter prepare the reader for the content of this chapter?
2. What is knowledge? And how do we access it?
3. Why/how does the mind perceive things as separate?
4. Why are words, symbol, and concepts not knowledge?
5. How does going beyond words connect to education and learning?
6. What is direct realization learning?

Perception is the function of the body and, therefore, represents
a limit on awareness. Perception sees through the body's eyes
and hears through the body's ears. It evokes the limited responses
which the body makes. . . . True perception is the basis of
knowledge, but knowing is the affirmation of truth and beyond
all perception. . . . Knowledge is timeless because certainty is not
questionable. You know *when you have ceased to ask questions.*
—A Course In Miracles

Chapter 2
Perception versus Knowledge

Niels Bohr, a pioneer of twentieth-century physics and 1922 winner of the Nobel Prize in Physics, wrote in his book *The Philosophical Writings of Niels Bohr, Vol. I*, "An independent reality, in the ordinary physical sense, can neither be ascribed to the phenomena nor to the agencies of observation" (1987). This Danish scientific voice echoes the Buddhist idea of dependent arising, the general principle of interdependent causation and its application in the twelve causes (*nidanas*). Who knew that a Nobel Prize–winning physicist would sound like a Buddhist philosopher? But there it is. Could it be that perception creates our experience of this world? Perception is an interpretation, a way to make sense out of what we observe as the similarities and differences between agencies of observation (subject) and phenomena (object). Perception is the disintegrating of information in an attempt to reintegrate it according to its own making. This is what the brain and central nervous center are doing.

Therefore, perceiving is the act of separating first, in order to piece back together in a way that makes sense to our personal awareness. Again, for a great academic exposition of this process, I suggest Peter M. Vishton's work, *Understanding the Secrets of Human Perception*.

Perception is the way our minds shape and translate our experience of physical reality. Experiences create beliefs, and beliefs create perception. When beliefs become fixed, perception stabilizes. Stabilized perceptions are the material that literally builds our belief patterns, our life habits, and eventually, our personal awareness. This personal awareness is what we believe to be all that is real. Now remember, neither the agencies of observation (our central nervous systems and physical senses) nor the objects of these senses (physical matter) can be said to possess an independent reality. Erwin Schrödinger, another Nobel Prize–winning physicist, in his book *What is Life?*, postulates the possibility that individual consciousness is only a manifestation of a unitary consciousness pervading the universe (Schrodinger 1967). This wholeness theory can be better understood in terms of looking rationally and empirically at what is knowledge and perception. This will give us insight into Niels Bohr's comment on the interdependent relationship of the agencies of observation and the phenomena that it observes.

The observable universe (only 4 percent) cannot be ascribed, as Niels Bohr said, in the "ordinary physical sense" an independent reality. So how do we actually *know* anything about physical matter? It is through our senses that we claim we know. We believe our brains and central nervous systems are our sole mechanism for verifying what we know to be real. They communicate our experience of reality to us. What we cannot know experientially, we believe or accept conceptually. We base learning on what our senses tell us as if those senses can tell us truly without fault. Our current educational model is based on a perception-oriented system, or brain-centered learning. Physics (though I must admit I am no math or science whiz) can tell us important information regarding our physical human reality. But it only can tell us what the bodily senses or our technological tools are capable of measuring or what we can believe or accept conceptually. What if the greatest information lies outside our physical measurements and personal beliefs or concepts?

Take the idea of quantum entanglement from the field of quantum mechanics: a physical phenomenon that occurs when pairs or groups of particles are generated or interact in ways such that the quantum state of each particle *cannot be described independently*— instead, a quantum state may be given for the system as a whole. This is the one idea Einstein refused to accept, making him one of quantum mechanics' harshest critics. The quantum world, dark matter, and dark energy are a mystery because we are unable to measure or quantify them and because we have no concept to imagine it. But what if we had another technology, a technology that could peer into the world beyond our physical measuring apparatuses? Our addiction to perception limits us to only accepting what the physical senses can measure. I believe we have a technology that goes beyond physical perception. Although perception is a measuring mechanism, it is not accurate because its very premise is change. A reality that changes or is not stable must by definition be an illusion. Illusions are made from perceptions. Knowledge is beyond perception because it is beyond change and processing and measuring.

Knowledge is what is true and certain and unalterable. This point is important. True or ultimate reality is what is occurring regardless of a singular perspective. If all perceptions are real, then none are true. What is true is the fact that we are all perceiving. But there is a difference between fact and truth. There is also a difference between reality and truth. Fact is what we understand about and describe of what we perceive and can verify scientifically about our reality. Reality can be closely associated with fact because it is based on what we can perceive, conceptualize, or accept. What we should call facts are pieces of current information about our reality derived through a process of science. Truth, on the other hand, is immutable and absolutely generalizable. Truth depends on nothing for verification. We know truth through realization not corroboration. Truth is constant, unalterable, and therefore, eternal. It is universal in nature which takes it out of the realm of human reasoning and natural law.

But we must also remember that knowledge is beyond perception. Perceptions behold only the replicas of the original. Beyond our personal awareness and individual intelligence is knowledge. But this reality is kept from us due to our addiction to the body's senses. Creative limitlessness is the natural state of our minds, which is why the mind is the center of learning. Knowledge is not something we obtain or conceptualize; it is a direct realization of the creative source. Knowledge is not an end but involves a process of transformation. This process produces thinking that is creative. Our thoughts correspond to the nonphysical aspect of brain functioning. Nonphysical energy makes up 96 percent of what "exists" in the universe and 99.999 percent of what makes up an atom. Our nonphysical world is the world that knowledge is hidden in. By reason, we can deduce that the energy that exists in the nonphysical form is the nexus of the next age of human education and evolution. As the center of our galaxy is a powerful black hole, at the very nexus of education is the mind. There is far more power and information that exists in the nonphysical form than in the physical form. Or we can say it this way: there is a vast amount of information in existence that we cannot understand as of yet.

David Bohm, who earned a PhD in physics from Berkley (and received his degree after his thesis was declared complete after being classified for use on the Manhattan Project), wrote in his article, "A New Theory of the Relationship of Mind and Matter," that "this link is indivisible in the sense that information contained in thought, which we feel to be on the 'mental' side, is at the same time a neurophysiological, chemical, and physical activity, which is clearly what is meant by this thought on the 'material' side" (1980). Mind is the "mental side"; it is not made of matter. But mind has an obvious energetic relationship with matter. Exploring the mental side of thought is the portal to a new education.

An important emphasis of a new education is that our minds participate in making real our experience of the material universe through thought. Again since thoughts are nonphysical, they are able to interact with nonphysical matter. David Bohm, an American theoretical physicist who contributed innovative and unorthodox ideas to quantum theory, philosophy of mind, and neuropsychology, called this precursor to physical matter the implicate order. In his book *Wholeness and the Implicate Order*, Bohm explains,

> In the enfolded [or implicate] order, space and time are no longer the dominant factors determining the relationships of dependence or independence of different elements. Rather, an entirely *different sort of basic connection* [emphasis mine] of elements is possible, from which our ordinary notions of space and time, along with those of *separately existent material particles* [emphasis mine], are abstracted as forms derived from the deeper order. These ordinary notions in fact appear in what is called the "explicate" or "unfolded" order, which is a special and distinguished form *contained within* [emphasis

mine] the general totality of all the implicate orders.
(1980)

I do not believe that mind creates physical matter. But mind has a creative influence on matter, and mind cannot be separate from the world of physical phenomena. The supreme quality of energy is that it seems to be both material and nonmaterial. Nonmaterial energy appears to be limitless. I believe, like Bohm, that nonmaterial energy is the source of material energy. A new education must examine the claim that mind is the activating agent for accessing what Bohm called the implicate order, where knowledge and creative thought reside.

When the mind is fulfilling its natural function as a creative agent, it is always doing one thing: bringing new evolutionary information from knowledge. From this viewpoint, what a new education would do is point the student's attention toward the end of a discipline, where we think we have exhausted the possibility of knowledge and purposefully aim our minds beyond that. A deeper awareness allows a new perspective because the mind no longer invests its energy into preconceived notions regarding any limitations in any discipline or area of understanding. Creative thought is seeing beyond limitations. Our minds have been conditioned to make hollow investments in stories that we or someone in our world literally made from perceptual learning. Instead of this, mind-centered learning focuses on the source of the creative power of the mind. The real function of the mind is creative thought, which lies just beyond our personal awareness. We are able to see something new of something old. Going from personal awareness to a broader awareness acts as a catalyst for greater mental cultivation. True mental cultivation comes from realizations that emerge from creative thought.

Perception does not induce creative thought. Perception runs primarily on pattern recognition; these come in forms of beliefs, bodily sensations, chemical reactions, and so forth. The unmindful repetitive attention that we give to this pattern is how beliefs are formed outside our conscious awareness. As this pattern gets played automatically and repetitively without our conscious awareness, world views and habits are built without our intention or attention. The power of the mind comes from its ability to energize thought with continuous attention. Attention then is a form of power that we possess and are in control of. Just think about this idea: The mind is powerful enough to superimpose a fictional reality that we construct automatically *without intentional awareness*. This unintentional awareness is the entire makeup of perception. This is why perception does not generate learning. You cannot learn what you are unaware of.

In review, knowledge is bound to nothing physical nor is it bound to any concept. We must begin to see that knowledge really starts with undoing errors in the mind or clearing the mind of illusions. Questions of what is true and false, real and unreal, and possible and impossible, again, become important to education. Knowledge involves the process of knowing the difference between illusion and reality. If our students cannot discern between the two, how can we expect them to learn or grow? What must happen in an educational process is that the artificial boundaries of our personal awareness must be made transparent. In other words, we must unlearn the habit of limiting our minds. Until we reexamine our idea of what knowledge is and how we achieve it, we will be missing a great opportunity to advance our young minds. Reshaping education is this generation's great commission.

Discussion Questions:

1. How does the quote at the beginning of the chapter relate to the content of this chapter?
2. According to this chapter, what is perception, and what is knowledge?
3. Why does the mind have two functions? And how does one utilize the power of mind?
4. How does each function of the mind contribute to education or knowledge?

If we fail to rethink and reorder our way of reasoning, we will continue to confuse data with knowledge, lose fundamental knowledge for living in society, allow experts to do most of our thinking, overlook the environmental variable in almost all fields of study, and wrongly assume that an increase in [information] enhances human goodness.
—Irene J. Dabrowski, PhD

Chapter 3
The New Education: Mind-Centered Learning

In the traditional education system, learning is derived from sensory interpretations and concepts and is nothing more than mental agreements, which produce perceptual learning. Learning is a temporary function of the mind. This is because we choose to perceive things as we wish them to be rather than as they are. Correcting thinking and adding substantial advancements to the discipline is the goal of the new education. When the mind reaches knowledge, it will no longer need to learn or perceive because all questions will be extinguished. All perception is really a question and interpretation about what something is. This is why knowledge must be understood to be a direct realization of creative thought. This is the natural occurrence of moving from perception to knowledge. Perceptual learning produces ingenuity and inventiveness, which are valued in this modern world. But both these, ingenuity and inventiveness, come from a sense of lack or a perceived need. Mind lacks nothing, nor does it rely on perception.

Our brains and bodies are learning devices, but they themselves do not learn. A device helps one to learn; it does not produce learning in and of itself. Learning is centered in the mind because only a mind can learn. Learning is what sentient beings do. Learning and evolving is the mark of sentience. But how does a mind learn? Answering this question requires a major shift in current educational thinking. Brain-based processing is not learning. The current learning model is based on perception and sensory experience as the two primary ways that learning takes place. Mind-centered learning is the way to creative thought through mental cultivation. A new education fills the student's experience with the creative power that comes from the broader awareness The purpose of education is to facilitate students' having constant unrestricted access to creative thought that proceeds from knowledge. Knowledge is the potential that exists in thought, and thought can either limit or create. Thought is powerful, and all thought has effect. The mind itself and the power that exists within it are the sole focus of the new education.

The goal of the new educational model is to place *the student's mental potential* at the center of the curriculum. This requires training and mental cultivation in order to achieve a new mind. In today's educational system, the mental energy of students is spent on memorizing information, preparing for careers, and becoming high-paid workers. This is inculcation, training, and conditioning, not education. Yes, students need to be prepared for the "real world." But if education imparts a skill or trade that does not truly prepare the student for the world beyond work, what good is that education once that skill or trade is no longer viable in the marketplace? Or what can a person do if he or she can no longer perform that certain job? Today's educational model seems to have become a work preparation academy. And this is great when one can derive real joy from one's work and this work adds something valuable to humanity. But this is not what the system of education is doing. The new educational model will help students learn how to experience ways to reach outside of the average idea into the realm of the creative.

The shift of a person's perspective is the primary path to knowledge. Ultimately, the mind must be able to break through the habitual unquestioned notion that *knowledge* can be conceptualized. This shift in perspective comes because the mind has let go of the meaning and value of perception itself. Making meaning and assigning value are great obsessions of a perception-addicted mind. It is well woven into our human DNA. Knowledge is arrived at through a process of shifting one's perspective. Knowledge does not *do* anything. Meaning that is derived from knowledge will only produce creative thinking. Creative thinking may inspire action. And yes, that thinking has to be converted into words and symbols to have any application in our life. But the means of conveying knowledge must not be mistaken for knowledge itself. Understanding this is the path to how one achieves a new mind. A masterful book, *Zen Mind, Beginner's Mind (1970)*, written by Shunryu Suzuki illustrates a wonderful Zen Buddhist teaching in understanding the beginner's mind. A new mind is like rediscovering what everything is. A beginner's mind, or new mind, allows us to gain access to knowledge, which produces creative thinking.

The most fundamental element of a great education is that it causes immutable and constructive expansion of the mind. Mental expansion or cultivation helps us go beyond our personal awareness. Education is what helps us to move out of perception and into knowledge. Once we pass that mysterious threshold of bodily perception, a creative spirit is awakened within the mind. We are effectively released from a limited understanding, the personal awareness, and allowed into a broader, more expansive awareness. We will no longer look at the world through a myoptimy (a singular-perspective belief system). This singular perspective *prevents* us from extending and expanding our awareness because it is based on the ideas of limitations. This belief requires that we see ourselves as separate from our environment and separate from one another, and ultimately from our creative source. This thought system is based on the separation of subject from the object, a dualistic reality. Therefore, this reality can only exist if the source is also split in terms of subject-object. The split requires that the mind attempt to reconcile opposite ideas within itself. In other words, perception-based learning reinforces a mind that produces split or conflicted thoughts. This split is what creates perception; perception is the foundation of brain-based learning.

The new educational system discussed in this book is focused on undoing this spilt and breaking through mental limitations. This is the direct realization process. A new mind is made aware of new possibilities that lay just outside of perception or personal awareness. And this is how a new mind is able to shift from perception to knowledge. This must eventually lead to letting go of attachments to conceptual learning. Understanding this is the beginning of mental cultivation. Concepts foster meaning for communication. They are communication devices, not knowledge. Mental errors like these can *only* be seen from a perspective other than the perspective that created the mental error in the first place. An erroneous thought can never correct its own error. Einstein was once credited with saying the world that we have made as a result of the level of thinking we have done thus far creates problems that we cannot solve at the same level as the level we created them at. Knowledge is a way of seeing without perception. In a sense the essence of the object and the essence of the subject share unfettered, unequivocal information.

Until we focus our attention on the nonphysical, nonconceptual world, we will not be able to deliberately access knowledge. Quantum physicists tell us that the nonmaterial energy that exists in one cubic meter of "empty space" has enough energy to boil all the ocean water on Earth. And it is my claim in this book that our minds have the creative ability to bring us into "contact" with this very powerful nonphysical energy source. Remember, in this world of perception the mind is a learning system and gives us access to our creative abilities. In fact, neuroscientists tell us that for every second (that is, one second in time), our brain processes 400 billion (400,000,000,000) bits of information from the body's various senses. Of those 400 billion bits per second, only two thousand are processed consciously! That is a ratio of 200 million to one, meaning most of us are only conscious of .000000005 percent of total reality. This miniscule portion of reality is what makes up our personal awareness. The vast amount of unprocessed information is still there, but we have not been able to access it. What is in that unprocessed information? This is why cultivating the mind will yield us a new world of possibilities, things we cannot yet dream of at this time. Most great minds will tell you in their own words that they made breakthroughs when they were not trying to, whether in the waking state of beta, alpha, or theta or the sleep-state of delta brainwave pattern. In the later states of alpha and theta, the thinking mind relaxes and gives way to the subconscious.

In his book *Brain Wave Vibration*, Ilchi Lee, president of the Korean Institute of Brain Science, he claims that through biofeedback these people were able to increase lower frequency alpha and theta brain waves, which are associated with a peaceful, meditative state of mind while controlling higher frequency beta waves (2008). Quoting Michael Winkelman, a neuroscientist at Arizona State University, Lee wrote,

This integration allows "unconscious and preconscious primary information processing function and outputs to be integrated into operations of the frontal cortex." In other words, the rational, conscious part of the brain is able to harmonize with the brain stem, the part of the brain dictating the subconscious operations of the body. (2008)

This usually happens by accident for most humans. But the new educational model focuses on *intentionally* creating a way to access more of the 399,999,998,000 bits of subconscious information. Because the goal of the current educational system is to sift through the two thousand bits of information, traditional education only requires students to recycle through old thoughts. Those two thousand bits represent static notions that we just simply agree on. Those two thousand bits represent our mass mind. This love affair with our own stories distorts our relationship with knowledge. The new educational model and the new minds are not satisfied with this goal, for the mind is more powerful than we currently know, and it is capable of accessing a greater portion of that remaining information.

A powerful example of this ability to go beyond personal awareness is presented in the book *Man's Search for Meaning*, written by Viktor Frankl (a prisoner in the Nazi death camps and Neurologist and psychiatrist and founder of Logotherapy and Existential Analysis): "In a position of utter desolation, when man cannot express himself in positive action, when his only achievement may consist in enduring his sufferings in the right way—an honorable way—in such a position man can, through loving contemplation of the image he carries of his beloved, achieve fulfillment" (2006). The ability to expand his awareness and extend his mind beyond his personal reality transformed Viktor Frankl's life while in the midst of hell. His mind reached into that great reservoir of knowledge and found creative thinking that had profound and measured effects in his environment. This power came from his shift of mental focus. It allowed Frankl to see the same tortuous situation from a new vantage point. This new vantage point brought new beneficial information to Frankl and those in his environment.

He was able to utilize the power of his mind to change his personal experience of reality by accessing creative thinking to focus on the affections of his heart, his wife. Beyond his immediate circumstances and environment, there was *always* that thought of "my beloved." He commanded his thoughts to stay on loving memories of his beloved. Frankl changed the hearts of his fellow prisoners and a few of the Nazi guards. This is the power of knowledge or creative thought. Frankl's story illustrates what happens when a person recognizes that the mind is causal and has access to a very rich power source. It reorders our thinking about cause and effect. Mind is experienced as and demonstrated to be the cause. What it "sees" are effects. This new mind affords us authority over thought and action.

In review, mind-centered learning is the process of removing limiting ideas and instead accessing ideas that come from the creative mind, which is the effect of shifting our perspective. The awareness of our mind expands as it regains its function of creative thinking. Our mental awareness expands because it receives something that is new from the act of shifting one's perspective. Mind-centered learning holds to the fundamental principle that the mind is the doorway of knowledge. Knowledge inspires creative thought only. We have to start thinking of the mind as much more than a conceptualizing tool. Our minds have access to knowledge, and knowledge is the source of our creative thinking. In our current educational paradigm, we don't understand or don't properly value the power of the creative function of our minds. While we dismiss or deny or trivialize this great power, we are wasting valuable opportunities to advance education to a place unrecognizable from our current vantage point.

Discussion Questions:

1. What is mind-centered learning?
2. What is the purpose of education according to this chapter? What ideas seem the most important and why?
3. What part do you think your "inner world" of thought plays in your learning?
4. How does the example of Viktor Frankl provide support for this chapter's claim about the purpose of education?
5. What are the fundamental differences between the current educational system and the new one being proposed in this chapter?

*Trainers give answers to students and want their pupils to do exactly
as they say. Educators ask questions and want their pupils to become
autonomous, to chart their own course, to surpass their masters.*
—Marco Navarro-Genie, research director,
Frontier Centre for Public Policy

Chapter 4
Definition of a True Teacher

As a teacher, I have much to learn and much to add. I tell my students
this: the fact that a person with a degree is standing in front of the
room giving out instruction does not make that person a teacher.
The game of matriculation, standardized testing, and gaining tenure
has lured some instructors into an academic psychosis. Issues of
funding and student retention have led some colleges to become
educational incubators. These two issues mixed with an outdated
curriculum have created the perfect conditions for change in our
educational paradigm. Teachers have been blamed and celebrated as
villains and heroes. Teachers, though, are only a part of the system
of education. They are on the front lines, so their jobs are always
conducted in a glass house. The pressure is enormous and heavy,
especially at the primary and secondary levels. And to those teachers
should go the lion's share of the education budget. Their jobs are
hard. But issues at the collegiate level involve more of the states of
mind of the instructor and the student. At that level, for the student,
it is about intention and choice. Most students at that level are
making the choice to go to college. So no amount of methodological

acrobats and fun classroom assignments can replace a teacher who is highly skilled in facilitating mind-centered learning among students.

These teachers are the masters at their jobs. A teacher must be an example of someone who is developing a new mind. In the teacher's presence a student can feel something palpable. The energy of the teacher is felt. These teachers have an unmistakable definite effect on those learning from them. In her book *The Charisma Myth*, Olivia Fox Cabane talks about how being present has measurable effects on those who are in front of us: "Now you know what charisma is: behaviors that project presence, power, and warmth. You know these behaviors can be learned, and you've been given an entire toolkit to do so" (2012). She says that this presence is a result of the mind being sincerely concentrated on the person or persons that one is with in the present moment. Supported by studies, she claims that charisma is made up of two main ingredients: compassion and presence. In the first few moments with a teacher, a student begins to feel a flicker within.

They light something within a student that becomes creatively alive, as my best friend Mike did for me. That is the power of being present with a true teacher who has her own creative spark already lit. The teacher is the hand that strikes the match (the mind) across a coarse surface. Imagine the match moving at a pace that allows you to see every single spark jumping from between the head of the match and the coarse surface. Those sparks are ignited as a student shifts his or her perspective from misperception to true perception. A teacher helps students achieve a new view of everything. Because this shifting of perspective is the process of learning, a teacher must be able to demonstrate the shifting of his or her own perspective. Teachers demonstrate this through bringing new insight or knowledge out of themselves and students. True teachers devise ways to tap the potential that is already within each student. True teachers bend students' attention back toward their own mental worlds. Therefore, an educator is a kind of attention-bender. Teachers point toward, make clear, and call forth the highest potential from within students, and then they facilitate students in recognizing it for themselves. Therefore, teachers aim their attention at students' potential to access knowledge for themselves. This is how teachers facilitate the process of mind-centered learning.

The paths of learning are as unique and as numerous as there are teachers. There exists no one best way to teach students how to achieve any standard of excellence. But there is one learner, and that is the mind. Focusing the student's attention on her inner world of thoughts, ideas, attitudes, perceptions, and beliefs is teaching. This is how a teacher bends students' attention back toward their own minds. Students must examine how those things in their minds affect the way they see and experience the world. They need to understand how those thoughts create the very perceptions and beliefs that cause limitation or liberation of that creative force. Only the mind can be aware of this. This awareness allows the mind to shift perspectives. Because the mind can examine the thoughts that it holds, it also has the power to change them. The power to change one's thoughts is the same power to create something new. Educators must begin to value this idea.

Students need to experience some benefit from giving an instructor their full attention, and it is that benefit that inspires students to keep giving their attention to the teacher. A true teacher will get the student farther faster. The teacher assists the student in shifting his or her perspective, which happens when one goes beyond one's personal awareness. The shift in perspective is really a series of fundamental steps a teacher helps a student to take. The final achievement of these shifts is the ultimate shift from perception to knowledge. In this state, the mind is constantly and freely accessing creative thought. Helping to develop this new mind is the primary intention and work of a teacher. Once students have a clear understanding of the power of their own minds, they can look out into the world of symbols and representations with new minds and see new possibilities.

True teachers devise ways to tap the potential that is already within each student. A teacher facilitates the process of taking a student beyond the realm of fixed possibilities. This work requires that the teacher is teaching from a broader awareness. A teacher is always teaching a student to improve his or her thinking and to be aware that there is more information outside of the student's personal awareness. Outside the fixed personal awareness is a world of knowledge, of new possibilities. Going outside personal awareness is a way to expand the mind. A true teacher draws knowledge out of students instead of attempting to place it into them. Teaching is more about clearing limitations than it is about instructing and information gathering. A true teacher develops mindfulness, and most importantly, continuously points each student back to his or her own mind as the ultimate teacher. An educator illustrates how the world that students are looking at cannot be separated from the things in their minds. New possibilities are what make new realities. This is the effect of awakening the creative function of a new mind. In our mind is where we create worlds and universes. The possibilities that come from this creative power are what change this world. So if there are parallel universes, they exist in our minds.

The new education comes from the perspective that every mind possesses the same knowledge and creative ability, but some, through practice and mastery, have gained access to more of that knowledge and are able to express more creative ability. Since all have within them the same knowledge, a teacher's function becomes clearing away obstructions (limitations) to knowledge and making students aware of new possibilities. True teachers are attempting to create tools that perform the task of cultivating pathways to that knowledge that lie outside of students' limited awareness. And then teachers walk with their student down the path, helping where necessary. This is the Greek practice of teaching and is the origin of the word pedagogy. Principally, the tools should have personal and relevant application for the students. If students cannot see the application of a lesson to their personal lives, it will be hard for that lesson to stick. This is what makes education useful to the student. If there is no practical, immediate, or relevant application of a lesson for today's students, it will be difficult to facilitate any kind of learning.

In review, helping students seeing beyond fixed possibilities and our personal awareness is the goal of a new education and true teachers. A professor must inspire the student to continuously return back to herself as her own teacher. It is not up to a teacher to motivate a student to pass a course. I will say it again: *it is not a teacher's job to motivate a student to pass a course.* If motivation is used, it needs to be used to produce enthusiasm about learning. Teachers must inspire students; they must spark within students a searching within themselves. A teacher must awaken the seeker within the student to meet the teacher within. A true teacher helps students essentially awaken and realize what was always within them. If this becomes a priority in our educational system, the area of study will make no difference. The application of this in any field of study is unlimited. The positive contribution students with new minds make to the world will be the fruit of a new education. And the fruit of a teacher is a ripe student.

Discussion Questions:

1. What is the primary job of a teacher?
2. How does a teacher engage his or her students?
3. Why is it important to make the lesson relevant to the student?
4. What is the importance of the teacher being mindful?

A Mystery school is . . . a school for the study of the mysteries of the inner nature of man and of surrounding nature. By understanding these mysteries, the student perceives his intimate relationship with [their source], and strives through self-discipline and devotion to become at one with his inner [teacher].
—Grace F. Knoche

Chapter 5

A Student Is Not the Same as an Attendee

The very denotative meaning of a student has been lost in this era of fast-food education, where the need to matriculate students and receive funding and hold political advantage has corrupted the system that molds young minds at the primary, secondary, and collegiate levels in America. The definition of *student* has become fuzzy at best. Test performance at every level of education is the standard by which a student is measured. So students become conditioned to memorize, regurgitate, and forget. Job/career preparation has become the ideal yardstick and expectation of our colleges. Most "students" are actually being made into attendees who go to school to pass a course in order to get the job that will provide them with a comfortable lifestyle. But creative thinking is not in their academic survival kit. Being a student is not about grades or being able to garrulously regurgitate facts. Education is not about rote anything, nor is it about test taking or career preparation. There is a difference between a student and a paying, registered attendee. The attendee has no intention of gaining command of the material being taught; instead, he or she does only what is minimally required to pass the class *without* learning. The attendee occupies space and does what is necessary to pass the course, if indeed he does pass. This does not make the attendee evil or bad. It is what it is. But there are core classes that must be mastered in order to construct a sound platform that provides stability for real students to leap from. These core classes involve information and skills that will be necessary for the rest of the student's career *and* life.

A student, by contrast to an attendee, is a sincere, earnest devotee of specific knowledge. Albert Einstein was a student. Marie Curie was a student. George Washington Carver was a student. Billie Holiday was a student. Duke Ellington was a student. Frida Kahlo was a student. Mozart was a student. Socrates was a student. Sappho was a student. Lao Tzu was a student. A student is someone who sets an iron-clad intention on gaining command of his mind and, as a consequence, of the material being taught. The student focuses attention on the lesson and then studies, practices, and actually gains command of the material. It is because of this mastery that a student can begin to add to the discipline they are studying. A student cultivating a new mind does all this in order to awaken his inner teacher, a way of becoming a master. A student is really a burgeoning master. Buddha is a master. Jesus is a master. Krishna is a master. Shakespeare is a master in his own right. This master resides within each of us. So a student is someone intentionally devoted to becoming a master. A prerequisite for true learning is the transformation of an attendee into a student and then of a student into a master. And practice and habit are what make the master.

Because that idea is so unfamiliar in education, students haven't been properly guided by the educational system to cultivate their minds. Mind is the learner and through its power of creativity can access something new. The mind is renewed because it sees the information and the world from a fresh perspective. The new mind is developing the ability to distinguish truth from illusion. When a student is able to access that inner source of knowledge, he or she will be able to discern truth from illusion. Having this discernment will help students understand that the limiting thoughts in their minds are illusory only. There is no thinking involved when the mind is under illusion. The larger world is thinking for us at that point. We have no clue as to what is real and true. Differentiating between the world thinking for us and creating with our own minds is the beginning of education.

A student who is developing a new mind focuses her intention on gaining command of her own mental world, especially her perceptions and beliefs about her minds. Without that intention, there is no opportunity for one to do so. Also a student gets into alignment with the intention of gaining command of the material *and* with the feeling of having command of the material. What does it feel like to study and understand the material well enough to teach others? How does it feel to be stress-free before or after a test? How does it feel to get the grade that makes you jump for joy and race to show someone who cares? Set an intention to feel those things and act in accordance with what will bring those realities about. When students act in accordance with an intention to develop themselves, they are giving permission for that development to come forward into their experience. This development is what allows us to shift our perspective and change our thoughts and beliefs. So, for students, the question is this: Can you give yourself a command (set an intention) and follow through with it? Once a student is in alignment with his or her intention, the change in the student's experience will be the effect of a new creative thinking. From here, it becomes important for a student to understand his or her relationship with the teacher.

Teachers have preferences, biases, prejudices, and desires just like students do. Each teacher has a particular way about them that requires students' special attention. This is not about brownnosing or kissing up to the teachers. But becoming aware of a teacher's proclivities allows students to gain insight into the expectations and standards of the person who will be preparing and grading their work. Familiarity with the teacher is about becoming familiar with the material as well because the material is shaped and disseminated by the teacher. Therefore, having a conscious understanding of one's teacher is equivalent to having a conscious understanding of the course work. The goal of the student who opens up this dialogue with the teacher is to understand the teacher and the material. What are the teacher's specific methodologies, points of interest, or major concerns? Knowing this information will help students to understand what to focus their studying on and what to emphasize on a test or assignment.

A conversation with the teacher before or after class can pay big dividends. The clear reciprocal communication between a teacher and a student is the only true methodology and is the essence of learning. But I must warn students to not make this a personal relationship. Sometimes students can help the instructor when there is a disconnect between what the instructor is attempting to teach and what the students are actually understanding. When the disconnection is ignored, confusion and frustration will run rampant through the entire class. This is why true students are necessary for education. Because of their investment of energy and their willful intention, students can become a corrective element for a lesson or a class discussion that is running perilously along; this is possible only when students have properly understood the purpose of both the teacher and the lesson.

In review, when students earnestly and sincerely search for understanding, knowledge will come. Knowledge rewards those who seek it by accelerating their meeting with that inner teacher, knowledge. This is the reason that the student sets his intention on true learning. All true students will tell you that at some point no one had to tell them to do their work or study or arrange their lives around their education. There will come a point when the attendee will become a student, and then there will be a point when the student realizes his own inner teacher. At this point a student will begin to add to the knowledge of the subject that he or she is studying. People will be drawn to you about whatever area you have decided to make your career. Information about the subject will come to you, seemingly, out of nowhere. This is the stage where you know you have awakened that inner teacher. This is a pivotal moment in the transformation of a student.

Discussion Questions:

1. What is the true definition of *student*?
2. Why is it important for a student to understand the function of the mind?
3. What role does intention have in someone becoming a student?
4. What is the goal of a student and why?
5. Why is understanding a teacher important for a student?

Consciousness, the level of perception . . . [makes] the mind a perceiver rather than a creator. Consciousness is correctly identified as the domain of the ego. The ego is a wrong-minded attempt to perceive yourself as you wish to be, rather than as you are. . . . [The ego] is capable of asking questions but not of perceiving meaningful answers because these would involve knowledge and cannot be perceived.
—*A Course in Miracles*

Chapter 6
A Mind-Centered Education: Ego, Time, and Money

The mind learns because it has the ability to access a source of knowledge that is unlimited. Learning happens only when something new, although recognizable, enters into the mind. Mind-centered learning is based on the principle that the mind is causal, creative, and the only learning system. Everything else is a learning device. A learning device's function is not to learn but to provide a way in which to learn. Until one ventures beyond his or her projections and interpretations and narratives, he or she will be stuck in a learning system that produces no more than average thinkers. The power of mind-centered learning is vital to accessing that sea of infinite information in Bohm's implicate order. This implicate order is what I call broader awareness where knowledge resides. And knowledge provides us with new creative thought that is actually outside the proverbial box.

Our physical bodies and our thoughts related to the body are what we identify with in our minds as being us. This limits the mind. Identifying with our corporeal experiences and all the beliefs that spring from this identification becomes the ego. The ego is *the* fundamental thought system that is based on perception and separation. This thought system is the sole reason we cannot access creative thinking. The fundamental issue is that the ego believes the body is sum total of our lives and our expression. When the mind is able to let go of the idea that it is limited to the body, the mind will reach into knowledge and arrive at a constant state of creative thought. From this, we will inherit a new mind that is restored to its creative function. The difference between creating and perceiving is the difference between all and nothing. The truth of this claim can only be experienced in a direct way. But until then, this brain/perception-based thought system is responsible for the limitation of our current curriculum.

The ego is the aggregation of ideas, perceptions, attitudes, and beliefs that you identify with as being you. The ego's main game is to keep you believing that it (ego) is the body and that this identification is the most important thing you need to focus on maintaining. The ego must keep you believing that the body is you and, therefore, is separate from all that is. Now this belief is the very nature of the larger world, so the ego indulges in making an almost infinite amount of stories for you to invest your energy into that make you feel like you are actually progressing as a life form—family, friends, work, kids, lovers, projects, theories, money, time, and so on. But the one constant is that we believe that we are separate from our world and that we are separate from other humans. As benign as this seems, this thought system infects us with the kind of thinking that cheats us out of our true creative function.

We erroneously think that we are separate from the immaterial world, and we remain unwilling to investigate that which could become the next stage of human evolution. This ego-driven thought system acts as a glue-like mental force that holds the illusory fragments of our story together. The ego and its subsequent thought system drains us of an enormous amount of energy. It also robs us of using that energy to think creatively. One of ego's effects is to lead us to invest most of our life energy into two major areas: time and money. As a matter of fact, an American saying alleges, "Money is time, and time is money." Money is not evil or bad. Nor is time good or bad. We use money to trade for our physical sustenance and survival. And we use it to fund wars and prisons and hospitals and education. But these particular questions become important in a new education: Do we really understand money and time? How does money really work? What is the reality of time? Don't worry—I am not going to go into a Keynesian explanation of economics or a metaphysical diatribe about time. I will focus on how intricately invested our ego wants us to be in making the stories of time and money seem real and important. And this is my version of a mind-centered education.

Money seems important because without it life appears to be hell. Those living in poverty are victims of the very "money" that we covet. Poverty is not the result of a lack of money but the circumstances that money creates in the relationship between people and resources. In order to see this clearly, we must briefly examine our economic system. The basic structure and workings of central banking systems, like America's Federal Reserve Bank, are keys to comprehending the workings of the idea of money. The current world system is operating on a monetary system that is regulated by a central bank. These central banks supply the money for most of the world's banking system. The Federal Reserve Bank (also called the Fed) is a privately owned bank that has no real oversight by any government agency. It is *not* a government institution. This means that no government agency has power over what the Federal Reserve does. (The very informative documentaries *The Money Masters (1996)*, directed by Bill Still, and *Zeitgeist: The Addendum (2008)* go into thorough detail about the workings of the Federal Reserve.) To truly understand the significance of the Federal Reserve banking system, we must give great consideration to the fact that the Federal Reserve is a privately owned banking system. Again, the Federal Reserve is not a part of the government. It is owned and operated by private individuals like you and me, and these private individual are the owners and controllers who make up the Federal Reserve. So when you read or hear about the Federal Reserve, think about elite people, families, and organizations. These persons, families, and organizations lend money to our government and our banks *at interest*. As we take a look at how private citizens lend money to governments, we see the emptiness behind the illusion of money.

The issue seems to be that the very monetary system itself is empty. The Federal Reserve has created a system based on fiat money, which only has value because of government regulation or law. In monetary economics, fiat money is an intrinsically useless good used as a means of payment. The Federal Reserve simply prints money out of thin air, trades it with the U.S. government for treasury bonds, and charges U.S. citizens for the interest those Federal Reserve notes cost the U.S. government. In other words, *money is an idea*. Along with fiat money, banks operate on a law determining the cash reserve ratio, which states that they are only required to have in reserves usually 10 percent of the money they loan out. This system is based on the fractional reserves system, a banking system which requires that only a fraction of bank deposits be backed by actual cash on hand and available for withdrawal. In other words, banks do not actually have 90 percent of the cash that they have loaned out. And the money they "lend" is actually not real in any physical way at all. They are legally able to charge interest on money that they don't actually have and never actually gave. Just like the Feds, banks are legally allowed to make money from something they never possessed in the first place. This is the exact way the Federal Reserve makes the money it loans to the U.S. government. The making of money and its economic effects are based solely on our imaginations. The actual dollar you hold in your hand is a belief in the value thereof. Money is only an idea that we give positive value to, at least for now.

The value we give the idea of money determines the health of the economic structure. An excellent movie that takes a look at the stock-trading side of our monetary system is *Inside Job (2011)* by Charles H. Ferguson. This movie does an excellent job of illustrating how the misapprehension of stock trading is set up and how it overfeeds on its own fantasy. What the Federal Reserve actually does is control our relationship to money. The Fed makes it easy or difficult for the general population to access money. It determines how much currency goes into circulation, how low or high interest rates are, what government agencies get funded, and which financial institutions get bailed out. The monetary system is like a million-armed octopus because its tentacles reach into almost every aspect of life on this planet. It is like a drug that creates consumer junkies and workaholics who spend their life's energy slaving for someone they don't even know because society demands it, and the current educational systems is a major culprit in this global scheme. In America, it seems as if we work in order to live, but it would be more accurate to say that we work and live to keep this monetary system alive. But as we take our mental energy back from the idea of money, we will do well to withdraw our belief in time as well.

Time is a jail where creative thinking lies bound and gagged by perception. This idea of linear time gives the sense of things progressively happening from past to present to future. The ego needs time in order to maintain the idea that it is a separate body. The concept of time seems very real to the mind because the body does age and eventually expire. I do acknowledge that we appear to get older and that our bodies do break down and eventually end. But that is not a result of time. That is the simple nature of physical structures; they deteriorate and transform. Physical entities require what is perceived as time and space to exist. The reality or substance of linear time as a real phenomenon does not exist. But if time and space are real, why do they not remain consistent everywhere in the universe at all times? Time is as real as space. Space can be physically altered by something as simple as the speed of an object or the gravitational attraction of a black hole. If you have enough speed, the distance from here to there will shrink. And we know that black holes bend light. *Biocentrism* (2009) by Robert Lanza is a great book that takes you through the science of these ideas.

Time is a construct of the ego mind. It is useful to ego so that it can get you to invest your energy into the idea of finality or death or oblivion. If you invest yourself in the idea of an ending to your life, which most people believe is physical only, you will urgently do all you can to find meaning or happiness according to the ego's standards. This is a game the ego plays because it knows you believe you are the body, which will have a finale. You see yourself and others aging and dying, so time must exist. But is this a result of time itself? No. It is a result of physical matter doing what it was made to do: make short-lived experiences. Time disappears when your attention is taken away from the belief that you are a body. When you play a video game or get lost in an ensnaring conversation with a friend or have an ecstatic orgasm, things like time, hunger, worries, and problems disappear.

What ego does not want you to focus on is timelessness, which is only contained in the present moment. We lose awareness of the present moment, which is eternal, because we get bound by time and space. This is why we feel stressed most of the day because we feel as if we do not have enough time in the day to get the things done that are required for us to live our lives. This *idea* of a lack of time creates stress in our bodies. We feel the lack in our financial lives. We need more money, so we work more. We need more or better friends. We see it in our physical bodies. We need to lose more weight.

In review, when our identity gets invested into time, we feel more limited to our bodies. That is why Viktor Frankl was able to feel love, joy, and peace while in the most severe and degrading circumstances. He was able to go into an unconditioned state where time and space conditions did not exist. Remember David Bohm's words : "In the enfolded [or implicate] order, space and time are no longer the dominant factors determining the relationships of dependence or independence of different elements." The very purpose of time is to bind and to limit, for that is how things get measured. Just imagine for a few seconds that you have no time limits and all the money in the world. Imagine for a minute that you know that you will not see death and will have all eternity to attempt to exhaust life. Doesn't the stress just melt away? Well, this is closer to truth for our mental reality than you know. And this is mind-centered learning. Education must generate avenues to access knowledge; education has to take students right up to the edge of perception and conceptual knowledge and encourage them to jump. This is the leap that a new education is calling forth.

Discussion Questions:

1. What is the ego, and how does it function?
2. What is the significance of the notion that time and money are only ideas?
3. Why does the ego need time and money?
4. What role does a new education play in understanding the "reality" of ego, time, and money?

Part II

Keys to a System of Writing

And by the way, everything in life is writable about if you have the outgoing guts to do it, and the imagination to improvise. The worst enemy to creativity is self-doubt.
—Sylvia Plath, *The Unabridged Journals of Sylvia Plath*

We write to taste life twice, in the moment and in retrospect.
—Anaïs Nin

Chapter 7
The Goal of Writing Is To...

I tell my students that I love teaching, but I *hate* grading papers. Imagine having to read writing efforts that barely make sense. And I am not being mean. I am being honest. I tell my students from the start of the semester that they must write as if their lives are literally hanging in the balance and the words they write are their only way of getting help. I ask them, "How clearly would you write that message, how concise would your message be, how simple would you make it—if your very *life* were actually hanging on every word?" Then I stress, "This is how you must write." Expository writing is an organized, structured art form. It has rules and guidelines and principles that must be respected. Writing is a science and an art. Here, however, I will focus on a "science" of writing. This system is written according to Modern Language Association (MLA) guidelines.

When I teach writing, I ask students if they understand what the goal of writing is. "The goal of writing is to . . .," I say, and wait. (I always go for a dramatic pause when I teach students about writing.) Then I ask students for ideas about what they think the goal of writing is. Many things are shouted out. The ideas are very close, but rarely do they say what I want them to understand. What has helped me become a better writer came to me by overhearing (okay, eavesdropping on) an English department meeting at my alma mater and by reading a great, short book called *The Elements of Style* (1959) by William Strunk Jr. and E. B. White. The goal of writing is to communicate *clearly* and *effectively*. It's that simple. Clarity is the structured, organized part. Effectiveness is about the art and careful use of words and their relationship to each other and the affect those words have on your audience.

If you had the *one* idea that would unite all mankind in peace for all eternity, what good would it be if you could not clearly communicate it? It wouldn't matter if you could understand the most profound insight into the universal order of things. If what you know cannot be communicated clearly, that vital information will not matter or make a difference to anyone else. It will be forever locked beyond articulation. As far as writing is concerned, an idea or thought is only as good as one's ability to articulate the information in writing that communicates clearly and effectively. Converting an idea or thought clearly into the written word is a skill that a lot of people who can already speak the language are missing. Writing English is like learning another language, even for native speakers who have spoken the language their entire lives. The spoken word has very few rules. A toddler with new speaking abilities can be understood. The one rule of speaking a language is simply that you have to be understood. Verbal communication does not need to be clear or concrete; it just needs to be understood. (This does not include public speaking or persuasive rhetoric.) The written word is another kind of beast, strict like a disciplinarian. The rules that govern written language are very meticulous. They require respect like the laws of nature. The knowledge *and* practice of the rules sets the stage for clear writing. In order for one to become a clear writer, one must study the rules of writing and gain command of grammar (the building blocks of language) and sentence structure (the vehicles of thought narratives), and one must practice writing as often as possible. Writing well can be learned, but it requires careful devotion.

One must develop the capacity to focus attention on the *exact words* one wants to use and on the thought one wants to communicate with those words. Writers must always be aware of what they are writing *as* they are writing. There are times, especially in creative writing, when a writer feels like his words are coming from another place and the writing is coming through him. Aside from those times, there must be intention and awareness placed on every word that is being chosen and used. When one brings awareness and intention to the construction of every word, phrase, and sentence, this sets the stage for clear writing. It is very important as well that a student of writing reads other skilled writers who produce good prose. No aspect of writing can be transferred to a student by a teacher. These skills are grown organically. Students must study and practice the rules in order to write clearly and effectively. Writing effectively comes only after one has command of clarity. Good, clear writing is accomplished through diverse diction, fluid syntax, and intimate knowledge of audience.

Diverse diction includes word choice, word usage, and vocabulary. Diverse diction is so important because word choice and word usage require the writer to bring her attention to every word she uses *as* she chooses to use it. You can only choose words you know the meaning of. Therefore, an extensive vocabulary is vital to clear writing. Your vocabulary acts like a bank. Either it is full of words and meaning, or it is lacking the options those words provide. Depending on your deposits, your options will be plentiful or limited. Knowing the meaning of more words makes you more capable of understanding and expounding upon more ideas. In writing, an extended vocabulary is like gold. It gives you many more options than those who have smaller vocabularies. Growing in knowledge and widening and deepening your knowledge base will ultimately shape your ability to write more effectively. If you study all the devices of creative writing and rhetoric but do not have a broad knowledge base, those devices will do you little good. Attempt to read widely and deeply in the fields that interest you. A breath *and* depth of knowledge will make your communication more effective. Drawing from different disciplines and various sources will give your writing a power that will have an immense impact on you as a writer and on your audience.

Word usage is the correct use of each word you include in any phrase or sentence. It requires you to use the correct word to communicate your idea. Word usage focuses on the way in which the word is being used in the context of the sentence. Does it communicate your idea accurately and clearly? If it does not, you have used the word improperly and must choose a different word or use it correctly. If you are not sure, use a dictionary to make sure. Diction is about knowing the meaning of the word you are using and making sure it is the right word for that phrase or sentence. Being this careful in your writing comes from mindfulness. If you care this much about choosing each word, you are on your way to becoming a clear writer. Word usage must be considered in the context of the sentence, whereas word choice is about whether you have the right word.

Word choice is about choosing the most accurate word that represents your idea or thought. Accuracy is not so much about whether the word is correct or not but whether it is exact. Ask yourself,

"Does this word *accurately* represent the exact idea or thought that I have in mind?" Accuracy is measured by the intention of the idea. The intended meaning is the bull's-eye, and your words are like arrows. This demands accuracy. If there are two or three words that you can choose from, first make certain you know the correct meaning of each word. Then check for any connotations associated with each particular word. Then ask yourself which word most accurately represents your intended meaning for that particular audience. This requires awareness and attention. Being fully present with each word is important, and this requires that you must also have proper syntax.

Syntax is the order in which you arrange words and phrases within a sentence. Clarity first depends on diction, and then it depends on the way you arrange words and phrases. Proper syntax also requires you to be careful about sentence balance. Arranging words requires the writer to be careful and mindful of dangling and misplaced modifiers. Even if you select the most accurate and exact word, placing it in an awkward or confusing order can kill the clarity of a sentence. Misplaced modifiers are exactly what they sound like. These are modifier (adjective or adverbs), usually in the form of words, phrases, or clauses, that are improperly placed in a sentence (Misplaced modifier: I went to the doctor sick and tired to see what was wrong with me. Correction: Sick and tired I went to the doctor to see what was wrong with me. (*The doctor wasn't sick and tired.*)) The way to fix misplaced modifiers is to place the modifier right next to, before or after, the word that it is modifying. Another issue of order is the dangling modifier (that is an awkward term, so I renamed it the unclear modifier). Its new name is *unclear modifier* because what is being modified is unclear. Sometimes what is being modified is left out of the sentence altogether, so it must be added. (Unclear modifier: <u>Showing them the house</u>, the carpet became an issue. Correction: <u>While I was showing them the house,</u>

the carpet became an issue. Correction: <u>Showing them the house, I noticed that</u> the carpet became an issue.) Another problem with an unclear (dangling) modifier is that the situation the sentence actually describes in that case is not logically possible. (Dangling modifier: <u>Riding in the back of the boat,</u> a shark attacked a seal. Correction: <u>Riding in the back of the boat, I saw</u> a shark attack a seal.) In both cases, you need to add the proper word(s) (usually the subject) right next to the modifier. The careful placement of words, phrases, and clauses is the very essence of clarity. With the right words and the correct placement of those words, you are on your way to clear writing; the other component of syntax is parallelism.

Parallelism requires that you place equal parts on either side of coordinating conjunctions, which helps balance a sentence. (It is important to note that things on the same side of the conjunction must also match each other.) For instance, if you have a verb phrase on one side of a coordinating conjunction or FANBOYS (<u>f</u>or, <u>a</u>nd, <u>n</u>or, <u>b</u>ut, <u>o</u>r, <u>y</u>et, <u>s</u>o), you need a verb phrase on the other side. Whatever you place on one side of a coordinating conjunction, you must mirror by placing the same type of grammatical structure on the other side. (Bad parallelism: She went running, jogging, and swam. Correction: She went running, jogging, and swimming. Or She ran, jogged, and swam.) The sentence maintains balance when its words, phrases, or clauses are grammatically equal. (Bad parallelism: I want to give her a ride home, <u>I will help her pack</u> [independent clause], and take her to the airport. Correction: I want to give her a ride home, help her pack, and take her to the airport. Make them all infinitive phrases. "To" is applied to all the verbs, making it an infinitive phrase.) The goal is to create clarity by maintaining equal grammatical structure throughout the entire sentence. Once you accomplish this, you will have command of balanced sentences. Clear writing is the gateway to effective writing.

With effective writing, you can begin to manipulate words, phrases, and sentences with the intention of having a particular effect on your reader. Every word, phrase, and clause is now a sword that you wield not only for clear communication but also for influence. Whether through creative writing, expository writing, or argumentative writing, you can now determine to a small but significant degree how your readers receive your words. There are many devices that are used to influence readers. No matter the device, effective writing produces an intended effect. This does not mean that you will always succeed, but it does mean that you will always have a purposeful intention for the words that you write.

An effective writer must take audience into consideration in a more thoughtful way than the average writer does. The familiarity with which you need to connect with your readers is absolutely important in effective writing. You cannot *assume* you know your audience. You must *know* them! This will give you the insight that is needed to craft your writing to affect the emotional, moral, or logical proclivities of your readers. You will know whether you need to focus on their mental or spiritual character, or you will know if you need to involve their intellect rather than their emotions. This knowledge of your audience's propensities will give you the insight into their thinking and values. Having this intimate knowledge will tell you their sensibilities and openings. It is from this place that you will choose your diction and order your words. It is from here you will know which allusions (references to things outside your writing) to make and which would be lost on a particular audience. This is when writing will begin to benefit you more than you can know. Writing is a science and an art. Both require the writer to pay the price of attention, awareness, and practice, without which he could hardly discover the freedom of creating art with words.

*There is nothing to writing. All you do is sit
down at a typewriter and bleed.*
—Ernest Hemingway

*Words can be like X-rays if you use them properly—they'll
go through anything. You read and you're pierced.*
—Aldous Huxley, *Brave New World*

Chapter 8

The Supremacy of Sentence Structure

The ability to use sentences to clearly and effectively communicate one's thoughts becomes most necessary in college writing. When a student acquires the skill of writing clearly and effectively, that student can begin playing with and exploring language outside convention. As students gain command of the ability to correctly (grammatically) express their thoughts clearly, their ability to think in a more organized manner is enhanced. But if they forget this fundamental principle of clarity, their writing is like a wild-spirited animal without discipline. *A student has command of writing sentences when her sentences have correct grammatical structure and each sentence clearly maintains the integrity of her intended message.* These two prerequisites are the gatekeepers to writing at the college level. It would benefit students, as thinkers and writers, to be aware of both sentence structure and the clarity of thought they desire to express. Students must learn to hold these two things within their awareness as they write.

Through practice and repetition, the rules and guidelines of writing will move to the subconscious mind like they do with driving home. You don't need to think about the rules of driving or the directions to get you home or to work or the physics of driving. You have repeated the act so many times that you can literally allow your mind to wander while you are driving, but still stay in your lane and safely get yourself to your destination. If you study, practice, synthesize, and gain command of parts of sentences and sentence structure, you are going to be capable of pushing the limits of conventional thinking and writing. It is gaining command of the science of the sentence that allows one to create poetry. The science of basic sentence structure helps one to understand the function of each part of a sentence. The sentence has three basic parts to convey thoughts. Each part has rules that guide its function. Understanding these rules keeps students from violating the function of each one of the three parts. The three basic parts of a sentence are phrases, dependent clauses, and independent clauses; the way you put these together forms your four basic sentence structures.

The phrase is not really necessary to a sentence because the phrase conveys ideas that lack a subject and verb combination. A phrase may have a verb in it, or it may have a subject (noun) in it. But it will *never* have both at the same time. A phrase is defined as two or more words that act as a part of speech. Note that a phrase is always acting as a part of speech: noun, pronoun, verb, preposition, interjection, conjunction, adjective, or adverb. A phrase will *always* be acting in *one* of these roles. But it can *only* hold *one* of these functions at a time. The phrase is a great tool to use as a qualifier. A qualifier is a word or group of words that restricts, limits, or specifies different parts of a sentence. (Example: In the house [prepositional phrase], there are two pillows in the closet [prepositional phrase] that I need you to bring to me [infinitive phrase].) Gaining command of the phrase will upgrade your descriptive and specifying abilities. A phrase is like a chameleon; it can blend in anywhere in the sentence in order to accent or to give detail to anything within the sentence. It is important to remember that a phrase must be *at least* two or more words, but it cannot include both subject and verb. There is no such thing as a phrase that is too long. The function of the phrase is to qualify a specific word, phrase, or clause in your sentence. A phrase must serve the function of one of the parts of speech, and it must be two or more words, but it cannot have both a subject and verb in it, as that would make it a clause. If you know grammar (proper use of the eight parts of speech), that knowledge will help you in discerning the difference between a phrase and a clause.

When a group of words has both subject and verb in it, that group of words is called a clause. A clause presents a "who" or a "what" (subject/nominative) and the action or state of being (verb/predicate) of that subject. There are two basic types of clauses. The first type of clause is a dependent clause. A dependent clause = subject + verb − complete thought. It is dependent because it requires something else to qualify it or make it grammatically legit. In other words, it would require something else in order to stand on its own. This is why it is dependent. A dependent clause is created when a subordinate conjunction or relative pronoun is attached to the subject and verb of the sentence. (Example: If my mother came home, she would kill me. [Subordinate clause]) *If* is the subordinate conjunction that requires that something more be written in order for the clause to make sense; otherwise, by removing *if,* we would have a perfectly normal sentence. (Example: My mother came home.) There are several subordinate conjunctions that students need to be familiar with: since, if, as, although, when, because, while, etc. The dependent clause has the ability to communicate conditions and relationships between ideas. (For example: If you ever cheat on me,

I will never forgive you. Example: <u>Because</u> I love you, I will forgive you.) Subordinate conjunctions like *if* and *because* place a condition on the sentence. All subordinating conjunctions place a condition on the sentence.

The other part of speech that makes it dependent is the relative pronoun; the three basic ones are *who/m*, *which*, and *that*. Relative pronouns, in a way, replace the subject in the clause. (For example: Tiger Woods, <u>who</u> is a great golfer, has had a rough time in the media.) The relative pronoun gives more information about a person or thing. A relative clause (<u>who</u> is a great golfer) is a type of dependent clause. "Who is a great golfer" is a dependent clause because by itself it would make no sense as a statement. It requires the independent clause (Tiger Woods has had a rough time in the media) in order to be complete and make sense. Now, here is a caveat. For Modern Language Association guidelines, you only use *who* when referring to people, and you only use *that* or *which* when referring to things. It would be incorrect to write, "My grandmother, <u>which</u> is dying from cancer, is turning eighty years old tomorrow." Without dependent clauses and subordinate conjunctions, it would be very difficult to give people ultimatums. All you would have are independent clauses.

An independent clause = subject + verb + complete thought. The independent clause is independent because it can stand by itself without any help. (Example: I have great health.) The independent clause can *never* have a subordinate conjunction or relative pronoun attached to it, or it would become a dependent clause. You can add phrases to an independent clause. (Example: Depending on the weather, I will either go to the beach or the mall.) But without help from the phrase or dependent clause, the independent clause can have no conditions. On the other hand, independent clauses are the backbone of all sentence structures. This clause is also known as a particular kind of sentence. There are four basic sentence structures, each of which has particular rules one must keep in mind when writing them.

The first sentence type is the simple sentence. The simple sentence = a subject + verb + complete thought, the same as an independent clause. (Example: Dark matter and dark energy are a mystery.) All sentences are vehicles for your thoughts, ideas, and visions to take form. So imagine that the simple sentence is a small vehicle, a motorcycle or Smart car. It does not have much room for a lot of stuff (ideas). You need to pick carefully what ideas you want to place in it. The simple sentence is constructed for simple, maybe even profound, ideas. It conveys your thought in a very simple, compact way. Proverbs or maxims are great examples, simple and concise. What is conveyed may be weighty in content, but it is simple and concise in delivery. Now a simple sentence will always contain *only one* independent clause (or one set of subject + verb + complete thought), but it can have a compound subject and compound verb. Compound just means two or more. So a simple sentence can have multiple subjects and verbs. But the rule is that each subject and verb must be connected by "and" or "or." (Example: Sean, Mike, James, Cindy, Kisha, and Lola ran, swam, and ate together at school. Note: Commas are needed for three or more subjects or verbs). As long as the same subjects are doing or being the same things, you have a simple sentence. A simple sentence must only contain one independent clause, but it can have phrases added to it. But again, in order for it to remain a simple sentence, it can only have one independent clause. If you add another independent clause, you have made another kind of sentence structure.

The sentence structure that has two or more independent clauses is called a compound sentence. A compound sentence is like a large truck; it can carry a lot of stuff but doesn't give you much maneuverability because it lacks the ability to include a dependent clause. The compound sentence has two or more independent (Ind) clauses joined by three specific combinations of punctuation. The basic way it looks grammatically is subject + verb + complete thought (necessary punctuation) subject + verb + complete thought = Ind + Ind. In between these two independent clauses, there must be one of three word/punctuation combinations. In no particular order, the first is the *comma* and *coordinating conjunction* "married pair." (Example: The US is a major superpower in the world, but America is going through a major economic recession.) The sentence must always include the comma and the coordinating conjunction together. Think of them like a married couple: what the grammar gods have married let no man tear asunder! The second option is only one piece of punctuation, the semicolon. This is the single guy or chick, but he or she does have a few rules: The first is that a semicolon is used only to separate two independent clauses. The second is that the two clauses must be closely related in subject matter, and the third rule is that the semicolon should be seldom used. (Example: Television and media attract the attention of hundreds of millions of people around the world; it would be hard for those who love watching it to turn off their TVs.) And last but not least is the one, two, three combo between the two independent clauses: (1) semicolon, (2) conjunctive adverb, and (3) comma. A conjunctive adverb (otherwise, on the other hand, however, nevertheless, for example, etc.) connects and continues the sentence. (Example: Freedom is the most beautiful quality; for example, feeling free makes me the most happy.) As many phrases and as many independent clauses as possible can be included in a compound sentence as long as it keeps its grammatical integrity. (Example: Love carries a potent force within it; that potency goes straight to the heart, and it causes powerful change within a person.) The only thing that cannot be added to a compound sentence is a dependent clause.

One or more dependent (Dep) clauses added to *only one* independent clause create a complex sentence. A complex sentence is subject + verb + complete thought and subject + verb − complete thought (only 1 Ind + 1 or more Dep). A complex sentence allows for conditions and qualifiers to come into the thought being communicated. This sentence structure is like a crossover vehicle. It gives you a little less room but greater versatility than the compound sentence. But there is a rule to know for this one too. If you use a dependent clause (S + V - CT) first, you will need to place a comma at the end of the dependent clause (just like I did here). You will *not* need a comma if the *independent* clause goes first (just like here). The main rule is that you can have as many dependent clauses and phrases as you want, but you can have only one independent clause. If you add another independent clause, you will create a completely different kind of sentence.

The compound-complex sentence is two or more independent clauses combined with one or more dependent clauses. The compound-complex sentence is like the ultimate sedan, sport utility, stretched luxury car. It can fly, swim, and even leap tall buildings in a single bound. This sentence structure provides the freedom to express all your thoughts and ideas into one sentence in a more complete and complex way. There is a range of ways to construct this kind of sentence. The three basic ways to build this sentence looks like this: (1) Ind + Ind + Dep, (2) Ind + Dep + Ind, and (3) Dep + Ind + Ind. You can have as many independent clauses, dependent clauses, or phrases as you would like. There is only a *minimum* requirement that you must meet. You can attach as many phrases as you like as long as you hold to the principle of clarity. The compound-complex sentence allows you to haul as many ideas as you can load into it, and it allows you to place conditions on the sentences as well. All of the punctuation rules are still in effect for this sentence and are even more important because the sentence structure can get quite long and complex. Here are three examples of the compound-complex sentence in the order I provided above:

1) Heroes and heroines are great for children's imaginations, and they can provide examples of good character and right behavior if the characters are the good guys.

2) Michael Jordan, who was the best basketball player in history, played the most graceful game I've ever seen; however, I don't think he was ever meant to serve as a role model for children.

3) If you ever find yourself in a relationship with someone you believe you love, you should make sure your minds and goals are compatible, and every secret should be disclosed.

This sentence structure allows you to say it all many different ways. Mastering and gaining command of the parts of a sentence, sentence structure, and punctuation will give you the ability to be successful in any class that requires you to write papers. All of this will take a lot of studying and practice, and the reward that awaits you is the ease of writing those long papers that those evil professors require you to write for that damn piece of paper they call a degree.

*I can shake off everything as I write; my sorrows
disappear, my courage is reborn.*
—Anne Frank

Chapter 9

The God of the Essay

The title of this chapter was a part of a lecture about a thesis claim that became the center of my teaching of writing an essay. What makes an essay different from a letter, an article, a report, a journal, a "paper," and so on? The training most of my students received in high school concerned writing thesis statements, which led to them learning how to write reports. The problem with this is that the students thought they were writing essays. A thesis, and by extension an essay, is a product of a student's very own organic thought processes; but what these students did in high school really did not require them to think or to be original. I tell students that, if they are honest about what they did in high school, they will see that most of them looked up facts and told the teacher about those facts in papers that everyone called essays. But that is a report! A report explains data or facts. A report is based on a statement and then provides the reader of the report with the evidence. Anyone can go look up facts and then repeat those facts. A report usually begins with a statement and contains little to no originality. A thesis claim and essay are diametrically different from a thesis statement and report. I show students the difference between a statement and a claim. A statement by definition is a declaration of something obvious. How can a student write an essay that is based on a statement if a statement is a fact? A thesis claim and an essay are joined by an inextricable bond because an essay is simply *an organized and structured explanation, clarification, and support of a thesis claim.*

Now we must get clear about what a thesis claim is. The thesis claim—not thesis statement—offers the student's particular, specific, personal observation on a topic without using the first person. A thesis claim is a specific, personal claim that a student will argue, prove, or illustrate in an essay using supporting evidence. Beginning with this redefinition of the essay, we start the semester with the emphasis placed on the value of students' thinking processes and ideas rather than the information they are writing about. Students come into my class with limited ideas about an essay or a thesis. They claim to have written dozens of them, but they cannot for the life of them tell me what an essay or thesis actually is. They guess and stumble around for some coherent idea, but they fail to give me a definition that fits the standard of a college-level essay. This is not their fault. Their teachers did not give them a clear definition of an essay or thesis. Instructors talked about how to write an "essay" and what went where, but students never learned the definition of a thesis or the overall purpose and structure of an essay.

Most of students' writing involved simply telling their teachers what they had learned and what they had read. They were never required to think or produce anything close to original work. All they had to do was go look up information and put it properly into their papers according to the mysterious MLA format. That kind of writing requires very little thinking. It is just laborious, tedious work to them. I am not for that kind of learning, if it can be called that. I find myself having to break students' faulty ideas and programming about writing an essay. I no longer allow them to believe that reporting is expository writing. What makes the difference in an essay at the college level are their particular, creative, critical, thoughtful, insightful, and maybe even, original ideas. When I teach them about creating their own claims for essays, they look at me as though I were the devil and just asked them to sign their souls over to me. The looks on their faces are priceless. The atmosphere changes in the class. What they eventually come to realize is that I am asking them to believe that their ideas are as valuable as mine or anyone else's. Again, an essay is simply an organized and structured explanation, clarification, and support of a thesis claim.

The essential difference between a statement and a claim is that a statement leads to a report and a claim leads to an essay. The reason this difference is of vital importance to understand is that higher education must begin to cultivate the use of students' minds. This is one of the main reasons why too many students dislike the educational process: it rarely values their thinking. A statement is obvious, requires no thinking, is based on facts, calls for no evidence, and leads to a report. This is the antithesis of a claim. A claim, on the other hand, is not obvious, is usually hidden, requires evidence, is based on subjectivity, requires thinking, and leads to an essay. This claim, which is a specific personal observation, becomes the god of the essay. Every word, phrase, sentence, and paragraph is dedicated to clarifying, explaining, and supporting the thesis. I have created a process and guidelines for a thesis, and specific terms and processes must be properly understood before I can go on to explain an essay and the god status of the thesis claim.

There are three distinct components of a thesis that comprise its structure: (1) it must make a *specific claim*; 2) it must *specifically* answer one or more of the questions who, what, where, when, why, or how; and 3) it must include enough specific claims to cover the page requirement (examples provided at the end). I teach my students to write this claim in one sentence; I also teach them to place it at the end of the introductory paragraph, which we will discuss later. The thesis also has three qualities. It is (1) clear, (2) simple, and (3) concise. This specific claim must clearly express the student's personal observation of one or more of the questions who, what, where, when, why, or how on a specific subject. This personal observation requires original thinking and must be organic, must require evidence, and must be based on subjectivity. The process I use for coming up with a thesis could benefit from people who read this book. If you have more effective means, please use them and share them with me.

I teach my students to first expect the process of developing a thesis to challenge their current mental abilities. Thesis development requires a lot of time and mental output. First, a student must decide on a general topic, like education. Then the student must ask himself the most important question, "What about education interests or intrigues me?" This question prompts students to become more specific and also to be more personally connected to their topics. Over the years I have learned that students write better when they care about their topics, so my advice is to make sure students choose something that they genuinely care about focusing on for the next few weeks. It becomes an opportunity for students to construct a major part of their own education. Attendees will not take advantage of this opportunity and will end up missing out on expanding their own awareness. But if the thesis process is practiced correctly, students will grow and begin to activate the teacher within.

The first method for creating a thesis claim is the question method. The student is to ask a series of questions that interest her regarding the assigned topic. The student is to consider issues that the teacher has chosen for the class. The questions need to be aimed at areas within the issue, topic, or subject that spark a true curiosity in the student's mind. The questions are like flashlight beams turned carefully in the direction of a very dark corner. When they write these questions down, the students will know close to nothing about the answers to these questions. The questions are purely a means to spark an inquisitive thirst. From these questions a thesis is born; these questions serve as the focal point of each student's inspired inquiry.

The student will then go into the second method I teach, the exhaustive-list method. The exhaustive list must be written in the form of specific and complete *claims*, not just one-word ideas. For this method, students imagine *as many* reasonable answers to one of the questions from the question method. The goal of the exhaustive list is to get down on paper as many specific, plausible, and creative answers as the student's mind can dig up. Do not be concerned about whether these answers can be proven or if they are true. Like a lawyer, the writer can either argue or illustrate his claim. A student doesn't necessarily need to prove the truth of the claim. He needs only to present evidence that can illustrate or persuade the reader of the viability of the thesis claim. Remember that a thesis by definition is something that is not firmly established but has logical merit. The advantage of this method is that students get a chance to take responsibility for their education and get an opportunity to exercise mental cultivation as they participate in their own education. Making these specific claims into the god of the essay requires time and focus. To start to pull everything together, students start with the first pre-thesis step: 1) grouping the specific claims into similar themes or categories; 2) the student picks his or her most interesting group from that exhaustive list.

With the specific claims already established, the student must make an overall personal proposal about the specific claims that he has chosen regarding the question he created. In a way, the student must piece these specific claims together into one general claim. The overall thesis claim should attempt to present a particular idea that has all three components of a thesis: (1) it makes a specific claim; (2) it specifically answers one or more of the questions who, what, where, when, why, or how; and (3) it includes enough specific claims to cover the required page length of the assignment. Unless the thesis claim has all three components, the writer does not yet have the core of his essay. The actual thesis claim requires students to put the rubber to the road or the pen to the paper and write until the claim has all three components and all three qualities (clear, simple, and concise). The thesis comes from a student setting aside time, going back through the instructions, following the process, and focusing his attention on creating claims from his own thinking.

Once the student has this one-sentence wonder, he has to take it through three critical steps to ensure that what he has written is indeed a valid thesis claim. These steps form the post-thesis process; this is the validation stage. If it does *not* have all three components, the student must find out which component is missing and then supply it. If it *does* have all three components, the student may pass go and collect $200 in order to move on to step two. Step two involves ensuring that the claim has all three qualities (clear, simple, and concise). This is the cleansing stage. The thesis should be as clear as possible, which usually means making it as simple and concise as possible. Simplicity makes it easier for the reader to be clear about what the writer is claiming. Concision involves getting rid of any unnecessary verbiage that does not qualify or specify the thesis claim. The third step is the outlining stage in which each specific claim is numbered. (This is also known as the breakdown stage.) It is critical that the student know and properly understand what he is actually claiming in his thesis.

The thesis is the standard by which the rest of the essay is measured. Without the thesis teachers really have no idea what the essay is supposed to be focused on. Students should not take this outlining step lightly. These specific claims will become the foundation for the rest of the essay. Once the student has identified each specific claim, he then forms topic sentences out of each claim, making sure each topic sentence is making the same claim as the thesis. The topic sentence should not repeat the exact same words that are in the thesis. Each topic sentence should use different words to state the same major idea and specific claims as the thesis. Together, the thesis and topic sentences constitute *essay* structure. The thesis and its topic sentences are analogous, respectively, to the brain and the central nervous system or the foundation of a building and its supporting structures; or as I like to say, the thesis is god/goddess, and the topic sentences are its sons and daughters. Without a thesis there can be no essay. After the thesis has been outlined and rightly divided into topic sentences, the writer builds the paragraph structure. I am borrowing Jane Schaffer's paragraph method to explain the basic structure of an organized, well-developed paragraph.

Some college English instructors may argue that this basic secondary tool is for high school not college. I do not claim that this is for everyone, but in my eleven years of teaching at the college level, I have learned that it provides students with a helpful structure in which to place and organize their ideas. After they gain command, I tell them to branch out to develop their own unique ways of organizing their ideas. For "College Writing, English 100," I teach the Jane Schaffer method as a tool that students can choose to implement if they find it helpful. Also at the college-writing level, I suggest that students expand and experiment with the structure to fit their own personal writing styles. I figure that, if students can gain command of a basic organized paragraph, then they, like me, will later begin to play with its structure and make it their own. This kind of writing process generates essays that are based on ideas that come from the student and are satisfactory college-level essays. The essay structure is the overall structure design, and the paragraph structure is focused on each unit within the design.

Paragraph structure begins with a topic sentence (TS), which acts like a mini thesis. The TS guides the entire paragraph just like the thesis guides the entire essay. The TS is the focus of the paragraph like the thesis is the focus of the essay. The topic sentence contains one of the specific claims from the thesis added to the overall major claim (which is why the breakdown stage of a thesis is so important). This topic sentence needs to present a subject and make a claim about that subject. Be certain that the topic sentence makes the same claim as the thesis but uses different words. Next is the concrete detail (CD), which is the supporting evidence. CDs are facts, statistics, quotes, valid logic or reasons, paraphrases, or examples. Students should keep in mind this caveat about using examples: there is a difference between an example and a scenario. An example is a real, historical, actual, factual happening, whereas a scenario is a fictional, made-up event that has no historical reality. The reason this distinction is so important is that students tend to use scenarios to support their claims; but because a scenario is not based in reality, it cannot be used as evidence. Each kind of CD offers the writer a way to give support or evidence or reason for her claim. The most important element of a CD, whichever the writer decides to use, is that it provides evidence for the claim in the TS. Without the CD, the TS is baseless and empty. After the supporting evidence is in place, the student is ready to supply the paragraphs with the most important material, commentary (CM).

CMs are the student's original, thoughtful, critical, insightful, creative ideas regarding how the CD supports the claim in the TS. Commentary focuses on explaining or clarifying how the CD supports the claim in the TS. Here is where students have to earn their grades. Getting students to understand commentary requires a lot of examples and comparisons that help students become comfortable with what thoughtful commentary looks like. Also, this is where practicing the skill of mental cultivation comes in handy. I always use this example to teach students about commentary. Chick Hearn was one of the best announcers in basketball because his game-time commentary was original, refreshing, and entertaining. CMs require creative thinking. Critical or thoughtful ideas take time to develop. It is the quality of commentary that separates As from Bs and Bs from Cs. If we follow the Jane Schaffer method, every CD needs at least two CMs. CMs represent the mental energy and time the student spent working on making her ideas clear and critical. Two CMs is the minimum; there can be more but not less. The one CD and the two CMs are the first cycle. Then this same cycle repeats with one more CD and two more CMs. Maintain focus on the TS with each cycle of CDs and CMs all the way to the end of the paragraph.

To close out the paragraph, the student needs a closing sentence (CS). The CS does two things: it concludes the paragraph, and it transitions the reader to the next paragraph. The CS gives the reader a sense of finality and a sense of what to expect next. I cannot emphasize enough how important a transition is at the close of a paragraph. It provides readers with a sensation of coherency between paragraphs like a smooth-flowing stream. The ability to finish a paragraph and introduce the next paragraph illustrates a level of awareness in rhetoric and audience awareness. These are the basics for each paragraph, and they should be considered a guide not the law. Students should keep in mind that this structure offers built-in organization and structure, which is why I believe it is so helpful in writing essays. But it should be used like training wheels until students gain command of the paragraph, and then they can make up their own versions of a well-organized and structured paragraph.

I teach my students how to write introductory paragraphs to begin their essays. The introductory paragraph consists of three parts (no surprise there, as I love the number three). Each part is about its functionality; the function of each part is vital. If each part functions as it should, you will have an effective introductory paragraph (intro). The first part and function of the intro is to grab the attention of the reader, teacher, or audience. My rule is that, if it does not grab the attention of the person who wrote it, it most likely will not grab the reader's attention either. The hook, as it is formally called, is creative and out of the box. It grabs the attention of the reader. It is flamboyant, clever, creative, shocking, unusual, surprising, critical, or brilliant. I encourage students to use their right to freedom of speech for this particular part and go for it! Usually a hook is a quote, statistic, fact, anecdote, or simply a word. But a great hook causes the reader immediately to invest attention into the essay. There is no length requirement. However many sentences or words it takes to grab the reader's attention is how long it should be. The only rule is that the hook needs to relate to the thesis in a logical way. It can't be so far out that there is no relation to the thesis.

The next part of the intro is the bridge, which connects the hook to the thesis. The function of the bridge is to prepare the reader for the thesis claim. The bridge is very important in shaping the reader's mind before the writer introduces her thesis claim. In the bridge the writer must provide background information on the thesis claim or build a contextual framework for the thesis claim. Background information should be included for claims that are atypical, exclusive, or specialized topics. Background information usually helps the reader to get caught up on the subject of the thesis so that he can be informed as he considers the validity of the thesis claim. Through contextual bridges, like a frame, the writer provides a way for the reader to view or perceive the thesis claim. The writer is shaping the parameter or context in which she is making the claim. Think of the way the worldviews of a given culture change context of a situation. If I walk up to an average American in a mall and say, "Damn, you are fat!," if he or she doesn't try to kill me, the person will most likely express anger toward me. If I walk up to a Japanese Sumo wrestler and say the exact same thing, he will take it as a compliment. Well, what changed? The social context changes the meaning of the exact same words. A writer's contextual bridge should do the same thing; the bridge is a long qualifier that limits, restricts, or specifies the context in which the writer wants her thesis to be perceived.

The final part of an intro is the thesis claim. If the intro is done correctly and written with careful, clear writing, it should grab the reader's attention, prepare the reader for the claim of the essay, and finally present the overall claim of the essay. Organizing an essay in this fashion allows for readers to read in a fluid, progressive manner while enjoying the ride. Following are examples of thesis development, theses, outlining, and essays from actual students who used my process for essay development. These essays were minimally edited in order to keep the student's writing as close to the original as possible. I wanted to maintain the integrity of their work. There are parts in the essay where brackets are placed around phrase or words to indicate rough reading, but these are minimal.

THESIS PROCESS#1 ★★★★★★★★★★★★★★★★★★★★★★★★★

Timothy Bright
Professor Marquis Nave
English 100
15 October 2013

Definition Essay Brainstorm:

1. What makes a genius?
2. Why were people who were geniuses given so much credit?
3. Where does genius come from?

Exhaustive List:

1. A genius is an individual that has extraordinary intellect and creative power. A C
2. A genius does not have a scientific measurement. B A
3. The term genius roots back to the Roman empire. A B
4. A genius can be defined by anyone who is extremely gifted in his or her field of study. B C
5. A genius does not have to be strictly defined as someone with a high IQ. B
6. A genius redefines the term intelligence. A B
7. A genius makes people look at things through a perspective that they never would have in the first place. C B
8. Everyone can essentially be a genius. C B A

- Genius is a person who puts forward a new bit of knowledge
  A. Brings varied viewpoints of insight
  B. Generates new forms of thinking
  C. Expands what's known

A genius, being any individual who offers an original piece of knowledge, brings different perspectives of enlightenment towards any aspect of intelligence, creates a new form of intellectual thought, and expands what is already known through his [or] her own ideas and perceptions

OUTLINE #1**************************************

Definition Essay Outline

Timothy Bright
Professor Marquis Nave
English 100
15 October 2013

I. Introduction

    1. Attention Getter
    2. Link to Thesis Claim
    3. A genius, being any individual who offers an original piece of knowledge, brings different perspectives of enlightenment towards any aspect of intelligence, creates a new form of intellectual thought, and expands what is already known through his [or] her own ideas and perceptions.

II. A genius provides fresh insight to the way we view particular components of cognitive understanding.

    1. "Genius." *Thefreedictionary.com*. Felix, n.d. Web. <http://www.thefreedictionary.com/genius>.

A. This gives the simple definition of what a genius is, and can be used to display how scientists view the word. It is said that a genius has extraordinary intellect and creative power.

B. There is no clear scientific measurement of a genius. It quickly can be used to go into the history of this word, which derived from the Roman mythology.

2. Berkun, Scott. "How To Be A Genius." *Www.Forbes.com.* Forbes Magazine, 2 Mar. 2009. Web. 10 Oct. 2013. <http://www.forbes.com/2009/02/27/genius-innovation-oreilly-technology-breakthroughs_genius.html>.

A. Explanation of why we look at geniuses differently from other people and how we disconnect ourselves from what it is to be a genius, and why we can be geniuses just as much as they can.

B. Geniuses don't exist in the present. Think of the people you've met: Would you call any of them a genius in the Mozart, Einstein, Shakespeare sense of the word? Even the MacArthur Foundation's "genius" grants don't call their winners geniuses.

3. Abrahams, Marc. "What Is Genius?" *Www.theguardian.com.* The Guardian, 23 Nov. 2009. Web. 10 Oct. 2013. <http://www.theguardian.com/education/2009/nov/24/improbable-research-genius-marc-abrahams>.

A. We throw the g-word around where it's safe: in reference to dead people. Since there's no one alive who witnessed Wolfgang Amadeus Mozart pee in his kindergarten pants or saw young Pablo Picasso eating crayons, we can call them geniuses in safety, as their humanity has been stripped from our memory.

B. How we look at geniuses and why we see them the way we do. What geniuses or people who have been deemed genius over the years have particularly gone through and why most of them have been through those sorts of circumstances. Why the same situations keep occurring to the same individuals and how it separates them from the rest of us. Or why we even glorify geniuses when they're really not that different [from] us at all. Or so it seems.

4. Closing Sentence and Transition

III. Geniuses produce a new manner of conceptual ideas and utilize them to bring about cutting-edge methods of thinking.

1. Dutton, Dennis. "Denis Dutton on Genius." *Denis Dutton on Genius*. John Hopkins University Press, 2010. Web. 10 Oct. 2013. <http://denisdutton.com/what_is_genius.htm>.

A. Dutton explains why geniuses think the way they do and the geniuses he's encountered in his lifetime. He introduces the concept that a genius could potentially be an individual who simply provides a new manner of thinking that the world hasn't seen. If intelligence is defined as the ability to acquire and apply knowledge and skill, then a genius provides his or her own form of intelligence.

2. Isaacson, Walter. "The Genius of Jobs." *NYTimes.com*. The New York Times, 29 Oct. 2011. Web. 8 Oct. 2013. <http://www.nytimes.com/2011/10/30/opinion/sunday/steve-jobss-genius.html?pagewanted=all&_r=0>.

   A. This article explains the genius of the late Steve Jobs. The author, Walter Isaacson, uses Steve Jobs as a way to explain what a true genius is. The information displayed in the article can be used to further define what a genius is by elaborating on what a genius does and how a genius thinks.

   B. It even uses the mind of Albert Einstein as an example. The genius can, essentially, be defined in the eyes of the beholder. Show me a genius and I'll show you a workaholic. Closing Sentence and Transition.

IV. Most importantly, a genius transcends what is widely noted and acknowledged as truth and extends what man kind is already aware of.

1. Cloud, John. "Is Genius Born or Can It Be Learned." *Www.TIME.com*. TIME, 13 Feb. 2009. Web. 10 Oct. 2013. <http://content.time.com/time/health/article/0%2C8599%2C1879593%2C00.html>.

   A. For all their brilliance, most geniuses did not live well-adjusted lives. Picasso, Van Gogh, Edison, Einstein and Nietzsche (and most major modern philosophers) were often miserable. Many never married or married often, abandoned children and fought depression.

B. Newton and Tesla spent years in isolation by choice and had enough personality disorders to warrant cabinets full of pharmaceuticals today. Michelangelo and da Vinci quit jobs and fled cities to escape debts.

2. "What Is a Genius?" *Www.wisegeek.org*. WiseGEEK, n.d. Web. 10 Oct. 2013. <http://www.wisegeek.org/what-is-a-genius.htm>.

A. Desiring fame in the present may spoil the talents you have. This explains why many young stars have one amazing work but never rise to the same brilliance later: They've lost their own opinions. Perhaps it's best to ignore opinions except from a trusted few and concentrate on the problems you wish to solve.

B. To focus on learning and creating seems wise. Leave it to the world after you're gone to decide if you were a genius or not. As long as you're free to create in ways that satisfy your passions and a handful of fans, you're doing better than most, including many of the people we call geniuses.

3. Michalko, Michael. "How Geniuses Think." *Www.creativitypost.com*. The Creativity Post, 28 Apr. 2012. Web. 10 Oct. 2013. <http://www.creativitypost.com/create/how_geniuses_think>.

A. For most of its history, the debate over what leads to genius has been dominated by a bitter, binary argument: is it nature or is it nurture — is genius genetically inherited, or are geniuses the products of stimulating and supportive homes?

B. Simonton takes the reasonable position that geniuses are the result of both good genes and good surroundings. His middle-of-the-road stance sets him apart from more ideological proponents like Galton (the founder of eugenics) as well as revisionists like Gladwell who argue that dedication and practice, as opposed to raw intelligence, are the most crucial determinants of success.

4. Closing Sentence and Transition

V. Conclusion

1. Concrete Detail
2. Closing Sentence

ESSAY#1 ********************************

Timothy Bright
Professor Marquis Nave
English 100
22 October 2013

Everyday Einstein

On March 14th, 1879 in the little city of Ulm located in the German Empire, a young peculiar Jewish boy was born to a salesman and his housewife. Contrary to the belief of his teachers, his parents knew that there was something different about the way this boy thought. When students learned the things their teachers informed them to know through the text, this boy would sit in the back, constantly questioning the theories and concepts that were being explained and would ask himself the question: why is that so? Even though he was born into an impoverished family living in a time and place that was of no assistance to his research, the boy never stopped inquiring and searching for the answers to these questions that continued to roam around in the vastness of his mind. This boy would grow up to be one of the most highly respected individuals known to man with an intellect that would broaden the very laws of modern physics, Mr. Albert Einstein. He was an anomaly born into the hands of indigence that never allowed his circumstances to interfere with the capabilities of his intelligence. Albert Einstein was a genius. But what made him a genius? Where did his genius come from? Why is it that so many people look up to this man as the trailblazer of contemporary knowledge? Einstein was just a man, but it was his mind that propelled him to become the icon he is today. It was not what he thought about that made him so brilliant but how he thought that made him the genius he was. In observing how this mastermind and others like him transformed human understanding by simply using a different process of thought, a clearer definition of just what it means to be a genius can be made. A genius, being any individual who offers an original piece of knowledge, brings different perspectives of enlightenment towards any aspect of intelligence, creates a new form of intellectual thought, and expands what is already known through his [or] her own ideas and perceptions.

A genius provides fresh insight to the way people view particular components of cognitive understanding. The term genius originally derived from the ancient Romans who used the word to describe a guiding spirit or a tutelary deity of a person, a family, or a place

(Dutton 3). The genius served as an intangible guardian and protector of whatever knowledge the individual, group, or location held and would insure that the knowledge was never lost. Essentially, since the Romans held fast to their theory that nothing existed without knowledge, then nothing existed without the genius. As the Roman Empire grew to its peak in the timeline of history, the "genii" would grow in strength and capacity. Since the achievements of exceptional individuals indicated the presence of a powerful genius, the concept of what it meant to be a genius evolved from a divine being to an actual human and his or her accomplishments by the time of Augustus (Abrahams 5). It was the original perception brought to a form of knowledge that made a genius stand out amongst the common people even in a time much before the twentieth century. The idea that "knowledge is power" was recognized long before Albert Einstein was even conceived, but it was how an individual took the knowledge to a new level that gave him or her the title of "genius." The ancient Romans recognized that if everything that was to be learned in the world never expanded, the world and life itself would never expand as well. Human beings are constantly searching for the truth and the truth slowly reveals itself through time. The people who search for and ascertain this truth in knowledge are the people who society deems as genius not because they are exceptional at knowing what has already been discovered, but because they have uncovered new truths. Therefore, the enlightenment found within any aspect of intelligence ultimately derives from the person who seeks to bring to light its existence. Renowned scientific researcher and founder of psychometrics, Mr. Francis Galton, further studied the concept of obtaining intelligence. Galton, being the cousin of naturalist Charles Darwin, yearned to find some of the unanswered questions Darwin brought up through his studies on the possible hereditary traits of genius activities (Cloud 32). What he soon discovered was that intelligence is ultimately something that is gained through practice and active seeking rather than a gift blessed upon someone at birth. Essentially, many individuals possess high scores in tests of cognitive understanding or IQ classification, but that does not mean these particular individuals are the people who will provide different perspectives of knowledge. Their brain may be wired to be high-functioning mechanisms, but that does not mean they have the personal willpower to come across new outlooks of reality and understanding. What this means is that there is no scientifically precise measurement or definition of what it means to be a genius. The personal drive that lives within an individual is what provides him or her to have genius qualities. Albert Einstein was not a genius because he was a high-functioning scientific thinker. He was a genius because he looked upon the process of scientific thought and brought a new perspective in hopes of expanding knowledge. He looked upon something like the concept of gravity and decided to observe its function from the unseen perspectives of geometric theory which [in turn] allowed him to discover the general theory of relativity and eventually that mass-energy equivalence. He sought out to view science in a way no one had before. That's what made him a genius. And in viewing things from a different perspective, an original thought process was formed.

Geniuses produce a new manner of conceptual ideas and utilize them to bring about cutting-edge methods of thinking. In 1921, a longitudinal study was generated to examine the development and characteristics of gifted children into adulthood. The study is entitled "Genetic Studies of Genius" and is currently still an active inquiry, making it the longest running longitudinal study in the world. The study was originally produced by Lewis Terman, an American Psychologist at Stanford University who would soon take [part] in constructing one of the most debated studies in history.

Terman yearned to disprove the then-current belief that gifted children were sickly, socially inept, and not well rounded. Not only did he disprove this notion, but he also allowed scientists to realize that the genius being held in each of those young minds did not derive from a chemical imbalance or a brain malfunction. What made each of those children gifted was their ability to bring about a new form of thinking that seemed to interfere with what was already known and intimidated the scientists of the time. To this day, there are scientists who believe such accusations were ludicrous and inaccurate, yet most of the children who Terman studied grew up to be leaders in the revolutionizing of industrialization (Michalko 22). What can be taken away from Terman's research is simple: geniuses, even from a young age, think differently from the way they are told to think. They create new forms of intellectual thought because of the inner desire they have to do so. In a genius' new and original forms of thought, different forms of intelligence are brought to life and new knowledge is soon discovered. An excellent example of such thought-processes can be found in the late Steve Jobs. The infamous entrepreneur, inventor, marketer, and founder of what would soon be the greatest technological company to ever exist started off his success simply by thinking differently. Jobs would often find fault in his education and knew the way his brain functioned was of a different level than that of his peers. He yearned to discover something greater than what was right in front of him which led him to difficulties with alcohol poisoning and drug addiction. However, none of those setbacks stopped his mind from thinking in a different perspective. In the creation process of the [A]pple computer which was held in his very own garage, Job's goal was not to sell computers and make money, but to expand the limits of technology through what he knew he could accomplish, which ended up being far greater than he could ever imagine (Isaacson

4). Steve Jobs was a genius and his legacy continues to live on with every Apple laptop opened for a homework assignment, every song downloaded on iTunes, and every text message sent on an iPhone. Yes, Steve Jobs obtained significantly high-test scores. Yes, Steve Jobs devoted his life to technology. But it was how Jobs thought and the conceptual ideas Jobs brought to the table that allowed his genius to take action. He, as well as many other geniuses, take their different processes of thought and utilize them to then undertake what geniuses do to change the world.

Most importantly, a genius transcends what is widely noted and acknowledged as truth and extends what man kind is already aware of. It has already been stated that the process through which geniuses provide fresh insight and cutting-edge methods of thinking is what propels geniuses towards their eminent success, but without the expanding of knowledge, a genius cannot exist. In recognizing this, discovering who exactly are the geniuses in this world becomes a much simpler task. Knowledge, being what man kind knows, is limitless in its accessibility. The individuals who search to extend what man kind is aware of are the people who can be given the label "genius." Geniuses are not just infamous artists like Wolfgang Amadeus Mozart, Vincent Van Gough, or William Shakespeare. They are not just world-renowned philosophers like Sophocles, Plato, or Aristotle. They are not just significant scientists like Galileo Galilei, Thomas Edison, or even Albert Einstein. The role of a genius serves so much more than just artistic, philosophical, scientific leaders. Geniuses exist today. Walt Disney expanded what was known to be a cinematic experience and transcended the limited ideas of creativity and imagination. Walt Disney is genius. Martin Luther King Jr. expanded what was known to be racially acceptable and took the idea of normality to a new meaning for a different generation. Martin Luther King Jr. is a genius. J.K. Rowling expanded the idea of what it meant to tell a fantastical children's story and started writing on a napkin what would soon become one of the most influential franchises of all time. J.K. Rowling is a genius. Mark Zuckerberg expanded the world of social networking and created a new form of general communication used by billions of people the world over. Mark Zuckerberg is a genius. Oprah Winfrey expanded what is known to be an icon and a symbol of happiness and wellbeing by actively being of service to others and being an example herself. Oprah Winfrey is a genius. These individuals are but few of a multitude of people who expand what mankind knows through their different forms of intellectual thought and active pursuit. They believe in so much more than what is exposed to them on the surface and seek to find the hidden truths that are waiting to be discovered to ultimately expand the history of the world and everything in it. So who, at the end of the day, is a genius? The answer is simple: everyone has the potential to be a genius. Everyone has the capability to see the world from a different perspective and utilize that outlook to discover something the world has yet to recognize because no two people see the world the same. Everyone is different, and because everyone is different, everyone can expand what is known through his or her own conceptual ideas. The problem is that not everyone believes this to be true. Some, in fact many, of the population believe that their mind is no greater than the one next to them and that their potential to discover something great is dwindled by others' accomplishments. This is simply not true. There is a genius that lies in everyone and it is an individual's duty to actively pursue what was meant for him or her to discover in this world.

Geniuses are everywhere. They continue to pursue the knowledge that has yet to be uncovered. The next Albert Einstein could be walking amongst humanity right now at this very moment. The job for mankind is to realize the potential each individual has and to use our perspectives to discover these new forms of knowledge. No one could have possibly said it better than prominent French intellectual writer and philosopher Simone de Beuvoir when she said, "One is not born a genius. One becomes a genius." This is the undeniable truth of knowledge-seekers today and knowledge-seekers to come. The geniuses are out there. It is the responsibility of humanity to become them.

Works Cited

Abrahams, Marc. "What Is Genius?" *Www.theguardian.com*. The Guardian, 23 Nov. 2009. Web. 10 Oct. 2013. <http://www.theguardian.com/education/2009/nov/24/improbable-research-genius-marc-abrahams>.

Berkun, Scott. "How To Be A Genius." *Www.Forbes.com*. Forbes Magazine, 2 Mar. 2009. Web. 10 Oct. 2013. <http://www.forbes.com/2009/02/27/genius-innovation-oreilly-technology-breakthroughs_genius.html>.

Cloud, John. "Is Genius Born or Can It Be Learned." *Www.TIME.com*. TIME, 13 Feb. 2009. Web. 10 Oct. 2013. <http://content.time.com/time/health/article/0%2C8599%2C1879593%2C00.html>.

Dutton, Dennis. "Denis Dutton on Genius." *Denis Dutton on Genius*. John Hopkins University Press, 2010. Web. 10 Oct. 2013. <http://denisdutton.com/what_is_genius.htm>.

"Genius." *Thefreedictionary.com*. Felix, n.d. Web. <http://www.thefreedictionary.com/genius>.

Isaacson, Walter. "The Genius of Jobs." *NYTimes.com*. The New York Times, 29 Oct. 2011. Web. 8 Oct. 2013. <http://www.

nytimes.com/2011/10/30/opinion/sunday/steve-jobss-genius.
html?pagewanted=all&_r=0>.

Michalko, Michael. "How Geniuses Think." *Www.creativitypost.
com.* The Creativity Post, 28 Apr. 2012. Web. 10 Oct. 2013.
<http://www.creativitypost.com/create/how_geniuses_think>.

"What Is a Genius?" *Www.wisegeek.org.* WiseGEEK, n.d. Web. 10
Oct. 2013. <http://www.wisegeek.org/what-is-a-genius.htm>.

ESSAY #2 ***********************************

Tara Ortiz-Payne
Professor Nave
English 100
19 Nov 2013

Pledging Our Beliefs

I pledge allegiance to the flag of the United States of America, and to the Republic for which it stands, one nation, under God, indivisible, with liberty and justice for all. Think back; do you have any memory of any of your classmates asking what the Pledge means or *why* they recite it? Probably not. Most Americans grew up reciting this pledge from the time they started kindergarten to the time they graduated from high school. It has been a part of one's daily routine for a good chunk of one's life, yet it is too often overlooked and given very little thought. Hardly anybody questions it. People go through with the ritual of reciting it for all of those years, but they are never taught where it came from, what it means, or why they say it today. The Pledge was written in 1892 by a socialist and former Baptist minister named Francis Bellamy for the celebration of the

400th anniversary of Christopher Columbus' discovery of America and also as part of a campaign to sell more American flags to public schools (Davis 659-660). Across the country, people fervently believe in the recitation of the Pledge in public schools. They believe it to be a symbol of everything the country stands for. Because of this, they fail to see the consequences of forcing schoolchildren to recite it every single day. The belief that American school children should recite the Pledge of Allegiance on a daily basis has the effects of teaching them to follow orders without question, subtly promotes religion, corrupt people's views on separation of church and state, and teaches children that the Pledge itself has no significance.

By reciting the Pledge every day, children learn to obey commands without any thought given to the meaning or the justness of those commands. That is because it is easier for teachers to simply teach their students the words and gestures and have students repeat them day after day. For example a study conducted by Eugene Freund and Donna Givner, educators at the University of Nebraska at Omaha, throughout several different elementary schools on social control in the educational system, found that many of the younger students either had no idea what the Pledge means or they guessed based off a word that they recognized (Schooling, the Pledge 19). There is too much extra work involved in talking about the Pledge and discussing its meaning, not to mention it is likely not even in the curriculum, so many teachers do not teach it. This lack of discussion leads students to believe that it is not important to think about the meaning of the Pledge, but they still must recite it. This plays a part in forming children's values, teaching them that it is acceptable to respect something that appears to represent American virtues without ever thinking about it. According to an article on the necessity of the recitation of the Pledge published in *Education Weekly*, a periodical devoted to education, the Pledge is recited every day, every year, with the same words, endorsed by school authorities and led by classroom teachers, "powerfully conveying to students that its recitation is the norm to which they are expected to conform" (Friends of the Court 1). In schools, there are always all kinds of speeches given to students, encouraging them to be creative, to do what they want and to be different. However, this is contradicted by the constricting methods of the educational system. The recitation of the Pledge is but one of these suppressors of personality. As a result of these elements combined, children become confused in during the crucial time in their lives when they are trying to figure out who they are. This confusion leads students to create the reality that they are only allowed to be themselves with authority approval. This reality hinders how a person expresses themselves and interacts with other people. One can carry this restrictive way of thinking for the rest of their life. If one adopts this mindless way of acceptance, they will be unable to see the darker side of things like what the Pledge really means and what ideas it promotes.

Because of the fervent belief in the daily recitation of the Pledge of Allegiance, religion is endorsed in a near invisible manner. With the inclusion of the phrase "under God" to the Pledge, this promotion is seemingly subtle, but still a very real problem stemming from the realm of theism. Most do not think anything of it and recite every word without even a hint of hesitation. Others, however, see it as a glaring issue that makes them feel discomfort because their religious beliefs are different. These people are shot down by supporters of the phrase who claim that the God mentioned in the Pledge is a secular symbol rather than a religious one. The article published in *Education Weekly* asserts the idea that while this concept could be understood by an adult, a 6 or 7-year old would reasonably perceive it as an affirmation of a belief they may or may not hold (Friends of the Court 1). As children grow up reciting the Pledge, they hear the phrase "under God" and assume that it means that God has significance in this country. If a student's parents practice Christianity, this belief is encouraged. Eventually, a child grows to value the supposed presence of God in this country. That person's reality now revolves around the idea that God is a major figure in American society. Since the majority of citizens in the United States practice Christianity, they see the phrase as proof that this country is a Christian one even though that is untrue; since the phrase has been associated with the Pledge for so long, businessman and active citizen of Estes Park, Colorado, David Habecker believes that reciting it would only serve to verify those assumptions even [if] the phrase in question were to be omitted (How I Failed 1). Without any attempt to teach children about the history or significance of the words of the Pledge, they grow up believing in the connection between God and America. This causes the number of people who falsely believe that America is a Christian country to grow. This one, simple phrase has the power to endorse a religion while blurring the line of separation of church and state.

Having to recite the Pledge of Allegiance every day causes people to develop a distorted view of what separation of church and state really means. When religion is promoted in such a manner, children begin to shape this mixture of church and state as a part of their reality. With the presence of the phrase, "under God" many people believe it is alright for the government to endorse certain beliefs. This idea has only spread over time and the American government takes every opportunity to take advantage of it. They use "God" to further national interests, from anti-communism in the 1950's with the addition of "under God" to the Pledge and "In God We Trust" to American currency to the war on terrorism in the 2000's with "God Bless America" bumper stickers seen on thousands of cars after the attacks of 9/11 (Davis 665). This type of religious endorsement encourages people to believe that America is a Christian country. When adults believe this, they pass that belief onto their children. With this encouragement, children grow up believing that religion and government are intertwined. When these children become adults, they believe religion is and should be a factor in government decisions. These people will value religious beliefs in government affairs. The very idea that such endorsement could be unconstitutional may never even cross their minds and these people will pass those same beliefs down to their children. The 9th U.S. Circuit Court of Appeals held, in a 2-1 vote, that even though students cannot be forced to recite the Pledge, "the school district is nonetheless conveying a message of state endorsement of a religious belief when it requires public schoolteachers to recite, and lead the recitation of, the current form of the pledge" (Davis 658). Since the Pledge is repeated every day, children have this endorsement drilled into their minds. It is done so subtly that nobody can see it and that is why hardly anybody is aware of it. When these children get older, they may make decisions such as who to vote for, based off of how they value the lack of separation of church and state. It is planting the seeds of deception early enough that it is unrecognizable. Those who do not conform are branded as unpatriotic outsiders and chastised by their peers. It is exactly this kind of behavior that goes against the freedom and tolerance this country boasts. This hypocrisy shapes children's idea of the strength and unity of the country.

The belief that children should recite the Pledge of Allegiance eventually leads to the realization that the Pledge is hollow. While the words may be recited over and over again, the actual ideas behind those words are not being carried out. Eventually, children will grow and learn this, thus weakening their trust in the United States government. From an informal study based on the inquiry of 20 preschool children who recite the Pledge daily, it was concluded "that the Pledge was not an effective way to instill asserted values in young children: 'Rote group recitation of the Pledge of Allegiance does not seem to be a desirable early method to use in helping young children grasp these abstract concepts" (Bennett 61). The Pledge clearly has no educational value, but children across the country must still recite it. The Pledge teaches children nothing but memorization and recitation, which are skills that are absolutely useless in helping children to become intelligent individuals. As children are made to recite it every day, they eventually go from excited and enthusiastic about the Pledge to apathetic and loathing it. As children become older, they merely recite it so that they do not get in trouble with the teacher. They also learn that if they choose not to recite the Pledge, they will earn unwanted attention from their peers. Nobody takes the time to really talk about the significance of the Pledge to students, which is counter-productive; many times, discussing something sparks interest in children. The way students recite the Pledge without talking about it is actually teaching them to hate it. According to Laurie J. Bennett, a doctoral student in Curriculum and Instruction at the University of Denver, "American students today can better use their time debating this question than marching in lockstep loyalty" (Bennett 63). The frightening part about this is that for the most part children never question this ritual. They simply repeat it day after day. This recitation slowly dulls any excitement or interest children may show in the Pledge. This is what leads to the apathy that can be seen today in older children and teenagers in regards to the Pledge. While many argue that it teaches students American values, actually discussing those values is a far greater teaching mechanism. This lack of discussion leads people to believe to be indifferent to their country's values. When one does not value their country, they do not care to research currents events. This leads to the ignorance seen in most Americans today. The time spent saying the Pledge could be better used, but unfortunately, it is not. The time used in reciting the Pledge would be better utilized by actually discussing it. However, nobody even takes the time to look at what some of the different parts of the Pledge mean. Take for example the phrase "to the flag." In the words of Warren Blumenfeld, author and editor of several works, it is "A mere piece of cloth. Like the words of a pledge, it's merely a symbol, which for me signifies nothing beyond the threads, the dyes, and the stitches holding it together" (6). Some may agree with this statement and others may not, but children are never given the opportunity to dissect the Pledge like this and figure out for themselves what they believe it means. When children learn to recite the Pledge without any content as to its meaning, they begin to lose interest in it. When the Pledge becomes nothing more than a rote routine in children's lives, they do not care about any meaning the Pledge may hold. It is at this point that the Pledge becomes, in the minds of children, meaningless and a pointless part of their school days.

Every morning, day after day, year after year, children across America recite the Pledge of Allegiance. Each one of those days pushes children farther away from being able to think about and understand the world around them. The nation is blind to this issue, so this corruption is allowed to grow. Even as time passes, people still strongly believe in the positive influence of the Pledge. In this country, *thirty-five* [emphasis mine] states have mandated that the Pledge is to be recited every day in schools (Martin 127). Why has it gone this far? Why is nobody speaking out about this injustice? The mindlessness that stems from reciting the Pledge of Allegiance only continues to grow and infect the minds of the innocent.

Works Cited

Bennett, Laurie J. "Classroom Recitation of The Pledge Of Allegiance And Its Educational Value: Analysis, Review, And Proposal." *Journal of Curriculum & Supervision* 20.1 (2004): 56-75. Academic Search Premier. Web. 8 Nov. 2013.

Blumenfeld, Warren J. "I Don't Pledge Allegiance (To Any Flag)." Humanist 73.6 (2013): 6. MasterFILE Premier. Web. 6 Nov. 2013.

Davis, Derek H. "The Pledge of Allegiance and American Values." Journal of Church & State Sept. 2003: 657. MasterFILE Premier. Web. 7 Nov. 2013.

Freund, Eugene H., and Donna Givner. Schooling, The Pledge Phenomenon And Social Control. n.p.: 1975. ERIC. Web. 10 Nov. 2013

"Friends of The Court." Education Week 23.25 (2004): 24. MasterFILE Premier. Web. 7 Nov. 2013.

Habecker, David. "How I Failed The Religious Test For Public Office." Humanist 65.4 (2005): 39. MasterFILE Premier. Web. 4 Nov. 2013.

Martin, Leisa A. "Examining The Pledge Of Allegiance." Social Studies 99.3 (2008): 127-131. Academic Search Premier. Web. 5 Nov. 2013.

ESSAY EXAMPLE #3************************

Joshua Navarro
Professor Nave
English 100
04 March 2014

Fat Hearts and Skinny Wallets

Saturated fat, sugar and salt are a few of the main ingredients in American culture. The mixture in America's melting pot is not racial and cultural diversity, but chemicals and artificial substances that is passed on as food. Somehow, different entrepreneurs throughout the years have come up with resturaunts that provide quick services and food that is prepared and cooked in a matter of minutes. Many Americans have experienced the convenience and quick accessibility of food through this industry, especially businessmen and workers who are constantly on the go. Although life has been made easy through these conveniences, this mass production and consumption of these products have made Americans unwholesome. The fast food industry has contributed to the unhealthy lifestyle of Americans. Most people are unaware of the hazardous content in fast food. They are manipulated by the unbelievably mouthwatering taste of these foods. These people aren't to blame, but the very anatomy [which what they] were created to be. Deliciousness and sensual aroma deceives a human body physiologically, psychologically and biologically. It goes against the very will of the human body; its consumption may be inevitable. The executives in fast food companies have focused their attention in greed and power in this capitalistic nation. Health is not a major concern of these entrepreneurs, but making a quick buck is their main objective. The fast food industry has majorly contributed to the obesity epidemic in America due to the cheap and harmful ingredients in the food, the manipulation of children into consuming their products, and the mass branching of fast food restaurants chains in poverty-stricken area that are populated with "minorities".

The fast food industry has caused many Americans to become overweight by feeding them food made with cheap and harmful ingredients. American society has fallen into the hands of corporate tricks and has replaced healthy food to [mass producing artificial imitated produced]. Food giants have been advertising their way into people's minds. Many Americans are consuming fast food every single day. One could even say that they have a strictly fast food diet. According to Don Thompson, CEO of McDonald's enterprise, he has claimed that he has lost twenty pounds while eating McDonald's every single day (Huffingtonpost.com). Although consumers may not even dare try this so-called diet, the executive is determined to make an asinine point. His claim does not detail any specific food or meal plans, nor does he elaborate more on what exactly he did exercise wise. How does one of the unhealthiest sources of food provide one with a well-balanced diet? It is undeniable that fast food industries do use a very small amount of fresh produce; however, most ingredients consist of additives and preservatives. Butylated Hydroxianysole, Caramel coloring, Yello 5 and 6, Acesulfame Potasium which are found in Ranch Dressing, Burger King's cinnabon mini rolls and apple pies and a plethora of soft drinks, and Sodium Nitrate and Monosodium Glutamate which are found in McDonald's burgers and chicken sandwiches, are the additives used that are cancerous and contain nothing but fat and cholesterol (Jacques Pg#). In fact it is impossible for the body to absorb any nutrients from fast food because of its ingredients. Many Americans are unaware or ignoring the fatal causes of consuming these harmful chemicals and hazardous meat substitutes. In the human body, the digestive tract can only fully digest certain items that go in the body. These different chemicals and cheap artificial ingredients are toxins that contain harmful carcinogens and are difficult to be digested. Since these ingredients do not contain any nutrients, the body turns the raw material into fat which is stored in the body. As fast food industries feed many Americans unhealthy products, they become obese. According to Karen R. Rios-Soto, a Computational Biology professor at Cornell University, Ithaca, New York, "During 2007-2010, adults consumed, on average, 11.3% of their total daily calories from fast food," which as a result more than, "one-third of U.S. adults are obese" (8). The increase of fast food intake in Americans has made this country an obese nation. Since many of the ingredients in fast food are unhealthy and harmful to the body, obesity rates are rising. The lack of nutritional value in fast foods, which is consumed regularly by Americans, makes their bodies nutrient-deprived. More fat and cholesterol is stored in human bodies than vitamins and minerals. Therefore, fast food has a direct influence to the causation of obesity epidemic. In addition to adding harmful ingredients in fast food, the fast food industry reaches out to America's children depriving them from a healthy future.

Americans are experiencing the obesity epidemic as a result of children being manipulated to consume the fast food industry's products. Children are the future of America. The next generation that stands before this nation will bring back innovation and great success in the future. However, the way fast food industries are reaching to young kids these days may stop America from acquiring [its] future successors. According to Don Thompson, the CEO of McDonald's enterprise, "If my kids want to have fries, you know what, I'm gonna let my kids have fries. If they are active and if they're moving, there's nothing wrong with having some fries. Burgers and fries are an American staple" (Polis pg#). He argues that health is mainly generated through daily physical activities and exercise. Although part of it is true, he is missing the major factor in actual physical health. Burning fat and calories can only help get somewhere so far; however, the body needs proper nutrients to sustain itself. Burgers and fries are not enough for a healthy meal. According to Michelle Mello, a director and professor in the program of Law and Public Health at Harvard University, "The most publicized lawsuit to date, Pelniun V. McDonald's was brought on behalf of children who consumed McDonald's products and allegedly became obese or overweight and developed diabetes, coronary heart disease High blood pressure, elevated cholesterol intake, or other health effects as a result" (208). Many ailments have been linked to obesity which is caused by consumption of artificial foods. McDonald's is still advertising to little children. Although McDonald's is the most highly criticized enterprise in the United States, there are several fast food restaurants that are known for advertising their "healthy" and "low-calorie foods" to children while pairing the food with toys and having fun, for example Burger King and Subway (Bernhardt). Advertising to children has caused them to desire and voluntarily consume their products. Children can be easily manipulated because of their lack of logical and rational thinking. Although fast food has become a treat to children, it is sold by fast food manufacturers as a reward for their success or excellence. Fast food has become the focal point for children who think that it is a reward for doing well. They are driven to do well in school or their choirs or obedience to parents in order to receive the action figures or dolls that come with the meals. Around forty-two percent of children in America consume fast food products daily (Paeratakul, Ferdinand 1332). Due to massive consumption of these unhealthy foods, children and adolescents who are "aged 2-19, more than 5 million girls and approximately 7 million boys [were] obese" (Ogden, Carrol 3). The manipulation of children into buying food products that lack nutrition and health value have caused too many American children their health, and having numerous fast food restaurants in one specific area only adds onto the obesity travesty of this country.

Many Americans are obese because of the rapid and continuous mass branching of fast food giants in chains, especially in low-income area that are predominantly populated with people of color. McDonald's has given voice to their strategy in acquiring more consumers: "McDonald's wants to have a site wherever people live work, play, or gather. Our convenience strategy is to monitor the changing lifestyles of consumers and intercept them at every turn. As we expand customer convenience, we gain market share" (Jekanowski, Blinkley 4). Convenience may sound like the deed of a good Samaritan; however, not many people know it is a corporate trick. This is a ploy to invade the customers' space by saturating their places of work, living, and socializing. Consumers' lifestyles are being co-opted by the ubiquitous presence of fast food in very places where they work, live, and relax. As time progresses, many people have assimilated fast food into their weekly routine so much that other nations see fast food and obesity as a part of our culture. Recent studies found that fast food restaurants are particularly closer in proximity to poorer areas that are populated mostly by "minority" groups (Quinterno 2). As a result, "38% of African American are obese, compared with 27% of Hispanics, 37% of Native Americans, and 21% of the entire U.S. population" (Quinterno 2). Most poverty stricken areas have poor choices of nutritious foods. The lack of supermarkets within these impoverished inner city areas has increased the obesity rates. However, convenience of affordable meals and restaurants in walking distances has taken a toll on poor inner city people. As consumptions increases, fast food restaurant branches increase as well, particularly McDonald's. According to the Anne T. Quinterino, a Policy Analyst at Mental Health Association of Rhode Island, she states that there are "approximately 33,000 McDonald's in the Unites States with 2,000 new ones added each year" (4). It seems like in every corner of every street a McDonalds, Starbucks, or Taco Bell is always open to serve nutrition-less food [to] the working class Americans.

The fast food industry, like a bully, has targeted those who have very few nutritional choices. They have found the ones who cannot protect themselves against the onslaught of advertising and convenience and cheap food items. Neighborhoods in inner cities are under attack, and no one is there to help, except the dialysis center that set up shop to reap the benefits of the sick and obese diabetes patients. America has fallen prey to the fast food giants. Obesity has now become even more evident because of the fast food industry. This obesity epidemic has changed the demographics of America: 31.8 percent obesity rate in the United States is second only to Mexico, according to a study released last month by the United Nations Food and Agricultural Organization (www.huffingtonpost. com). Does business trump health? The future of health in America is at stake. The foundation set for these future scholars and innovators are burgers and fries. These children are, unknowingly, sowing into an unhealthy future.

OUTLINE #2************************************

Miles Arambulo
Professor Nave
English 52
11 October 2013

Homeschooled America

I. Thesis: Homeschooling in America is the prime educational system for high school teenagers because homeschoolers are academically superb, they are involved with the community, and the morals of the students are spectacular.

II. Topic Sentence #1: The top educational system in America for high school teenagers is homeschooling because they are well rounded academically.

    a. CD: A majority of homeschoolers attained an above average test score on SAT's

    b. CD: An increased number of colleges in American prefer homeschoolers to enroll in their schools.

III. Topic Sentence #2: As being trained academically in homeschooling, which is the best educational system in America, part of their duty is to involve themselves in communities.

    a. CD: Homeschoolers serve in homeless shelters and rescue missions to help society.

    b. CD: Seventy-one percent of home school graduates participate in ongoing community service activities, including politics, compared to 37% of adults in similar ages.

IV. Topic Sentence #3: Aside from being a member of the leading educational system in America, homeschoolers possess outstanding moral values that show discipline and maturity.

    a. CD: Homeschoolers have good self-esteem because they are highly encouraged to be themselves.

    b. CD: Homeschoolers are exposed to a wider variety of people and social situations.

ESSAY EXAMPLE #4************************

Miles Arambulo
Professor Nave
Eng. 52
21 October 2013

Home Bona Fide Enlightenment

"Homeschooled people are stupid, retarded, religious freaks who don't have a life. Bullying is a part of growing up!" are a few things so-called normal teenagers who attend public or private schools in America say to the poor group of homeschoolers. It is tough to completely understand why the general public treat and identify all homeschooled kids and teenagers as weird or anti-social. They are just ordinary human beings like everyone else. Some are nerds, some are mentally challenged, some are jocks, and some are not socialized. That is just the way it is because everyone is different in their own unique way. People easily forget what truly matters. Homeschooling gets the job done, and it is why every year the number of homeschooled students increase 7 to 15 percent (hslda. org). the homeschooled students deserve much more credit for their achievements they have accomplished for the past few years. Homeschooling in America is the prime educational system for middle school and high school students because homeschoolers are academically superb, they are involved within the community, and the morals of the students are spectacular.

The top educational system in America for high school teenagers is homeschooling because they are well rounded academically. After conducting an academic exam to test homeschoolers' knowledge in 1998, Dr. Laerence Rudner, Director of the ERIC Clearinghouse on Assessment and Evaluation, discovered, "Almost 25 percent of homeschooled students tested are enrolled in one or more grades above their age-level peers in traditional public and private schools," (Rudner 32). Because of having the freedom to gather information in a pace where the student is comfortable, the students' potential to reach a higher level of education is increased regardless of the completed education level of the instructed parents, guardians, or tutor who teaches them. Homeschoolers never fail to prove the critical public wrong when it comes down to statistics. An increased number of colleges are starting [to] recognize homeschoolers because they are proved to be hard workers: "A study of 2,219 students who reported their homeschooled status on the SAT in 1999 showed that [these] students scored on average of 1083—67 points above the national average of 1016" (www.eric.ed.gov). Homeschoolers have consistently prepared themselves for college. Earning an above average SAT score is impressive no matter what middle school and high school attended. Since homeschoolers are focused on learning, they balance their time between improving academic abilities and participating in group activities.

While being trained academically in homeschooling, which is the best educational system in America, homeschoolers greatly include themselves in communities. According to the Home School Legal Defense Association, a nonprofit advocacy organization for homeschool students since 1983, homeschool graduates have continuously been committed in giving back to the community: "Seventy-one percent participate in an ongoing community service activity (e.g., coaching a sports team, volunteering at a school, or working with a church or neighborhood association), compared to 37% of U.S. adults of similar ages" (hsdla.org). Whoever thought homeschoolers and their graduates have been generously serving the community for many years now? Volunteering in communities has strengthened the bond between homeschoolers and society. Kathryn Chandler and Stephen P. Broughman of National Center for Education Statistics, and Stacey Bielick of Education Statistics Institute studied that homeschoolers have developed a solid connection with other schools: "Public schools or school districts sometimes offer support for homeschoolers by providing parents with a curriculum, books, and material, places to meet, and the opportunity for homeschooled children to attend classes and participate in extracurricular activities at the school" (Bielick, Chandler, Broughman 19). With all these new resources given to homeschoolers, there is no wonder why they excel among other students. The extracurricular opportunities given to homeschoolers have been valued in many ways. One has a chance to interact with other students of different ages while learning how to socialize in a sophisticated manner.

Aside from being a member of the leading educational system in America, homeschoolers possess outstanding moral and maturity. Parents play a big role in mentoring children's behavior: "Finding indicated that homeschooling parents had more hands-on involvement in their child's education" (ERIC.ed.gov). These parents mold their children's mind with motivation and good self-esteem. Students who are motivated with beliefs are more often able to reach success and develop high self-esteem because they acquire a better outlook on life which makes them more mature among other kids and teens. Studies show that the first generation of homeschoolers (1980's) are happier, more content financially and job-wise have a better perspective in life and believes that success comes from hard work (hsdla.org). Success is achieved when one is satisfied with what they have. In this statistic, homeschoolers proved everyone that all the hard work they've put in has finally paid off.

While everyone else is busy criticizing them, homeschoolers have been absorbing all the hate while focusing on enhancing their outlook on life. In homeschooling, education is always the main priority. The first batch of American homeschoolers are satisfied with how their personal lives have turned out after being academically, socially, and mentally educated through homeschooling (hsdla.org). Aside from being well educated, the students also learn how to work hard and bring their 100% in everything they do. The true winners in life are not those who are highly paid and tired of working. The true winners in life are those people who are satisfied and happy with what they have and what they have become. Who does not want their children to be both successful and happy? If parents care so much on how their children would grow up, why not consider homeschooling? Sacrificing a little bit of personal time to educate their children thoroughly won't hurt. Homeschooling continues to prove that it is the top education out there for the young children of America. It is about time to drop the criticism and start showing appreciation of what homeschooling have accomplished in the past few decades.

Works Cited

Rudner, Lawrence M. "Scholastic Achievement and Demographic Characteristics of Home School Students in 1998." EducationPolicy Analysis Archives. V7. (1999): 39. ERIC. Web. 23 October 2013.

Lips, Dan; Feinberg, Evan. "Homeschooling: A Growing Option in American Education." *Backgrounder*. 2122. (2008): 8. ERIC. Web. 21 October. 2013.

Ray, Brian. "Homeschooling Grows Up" *hala.org*. 2003. Web. 21 October. 2013.

Beilick, Stacey: Chandler, Kathryn: Broughman, Stephen. "Homeschooling in the United States: 1999" NCES 2001033, (2001):30. NCES. Web. 21 October. 2013.

Groover, Susan Varner; Endsley, Richard C.: "Family Environment and Attitudes of Homeschoolers and Non-Homeschoolers." ERIC 34pp. (1988): 34. ERIC. Web. 21 October. 2013.

END OF EXAMPLES★★★★★★★★★★★★★★★★★★★★★★★★★★★★

Chapter 10
Grammar Plain and Simple

My generation had *Schoolhouse Rock*. Grammar was a part of our regular TV programming. Although, I must admit that I never related *Schoolhouse Rock* to my schoolwork, which is probably why I felt incapable of expressing myself in writing until the day I took a grammar course in college. Learning the eight parts of speech is essential for beginning writers. I have come across many types of writers and their issues and have noticed a few things. When students grasp the definition, function, and proper usage of the eight parts of speech, their writing improves. This chapter is not comprehensive. I am no grammarian. The chapter covers the basic knowledge and skills that are necessary to write clear and effective sentences and compose a college-level essay. Understanding how to use each part of speech properly is the point of this chapter. In order to understand parts of speech, students need to memorize their definitions and understand their functions within the context of a sentence. The relationship between definition and function is vital to really being able to correctly use the eight parts of speech.

Grammar seems to be some kind of abstraction for my students, a mysterious fog that has inexplicably clung to them since elementary school; but it is simply the eight parts of speech. When schools say they are teaching grammar, they are attempting to teach their students the definitions, functions, and usage of the parts of speech. These eight parts of speech are the building blocks of our written language. Grammar, according to the Encarta dictionary, is defined as "the system of rules by which words are formed and put together to make sentences." The eight parts of speech are: nouns, pronouns, verbs, conjunctions (there are two types), adverbs, adjectives, prepositions, and interjections. The eight parts of speech are the eight major building blocks of the English language. These pieces function together to communicate one's ideas in a clear, coherent, and organized fashion. The eight parts of speech work through the forms of words, phrases, clauses, and sentences. Here I will first define each part of speech and then discuss how it functions in a sentence and then examine its proper usage.

Noun:

- Definition: a naming word (or group of words).
- Function: used as the name of a class of people, places, or things.
- Proper usage: <u>Today</u> is a beautiful <u>day</u>. My <u>nana</u> is coming over to babysit me.

Pronoun:

- Definition: a word that replaces a noun.
- Function: substitutes for a noun or a noun phrase, e.g. *I, you, them, it, ours.*
- Proper usage: <u>I</u> do not like <u>it</u> when people <u>I</u> don't know send <u>me</u> friend requests on Facebook.

- **Indefinite Pronoun:**

  o Definition: an unspecified pronoun.
  o Function: refers to a nonspecific person or thing, e.g. *someone*, *nothing*, or *anything*.
  o Proper usage: Tell me what you want, <u>anything</u> at all.

- **Relative Pronoun:**

  o Definition: a pronoun that replaces a noun and introduces a relative clause.
  o Function: refers to a previously used noun and introduces a relative clause, e.g. *that*, *which*, or *who/m*.

    ▪ Use *who* or *whom* when referring to people, and use *that* or *which* when referring to things.

  o Proper usage: Tiger Woods, <u>who</u> is arguably the greatest golfer in history, has had a very tough time in the media lately.

    ▪ Use *who* when it is in the subjective position of the sentence and *whom* when it is in the objective position of the sentence.

      • *Subjective* means that it is acting on a verb (example above).
      • *Objective* means that it is being acted upon.

    ▪ Proper Usage: I am intrigued by Eden-Simone and Marquis <u>whom</u> I think about all day.

Verb:

- Definition: a word that expresses a state of being or an action.
- Function: shows that an action is taking place or indicates the existence of a state or condition.
- Proper usage: I <u>am</u> here. (The word *am* indicates a present state of being.) I <u>voted</u> in the elections yesterday. (*Voted* is the action.)
- There are compound verbs and verb phrases.

  o Compound verbs are two or more verbs that must be connected by *and* or *or.*

    ▪ Example: Shela <u>caught</u> bronchitis **and** <u>spread</u> it to her friends.

  o Verb phrases are the main verb + the helping verb. A helping verb assists with placing the verb in the past, present progressive, or future tense.

    ▪ Example: I <u>should have been</u> a better friend to Mike.

*Verbal:

- Although verbals are not a particular one of the eight parts of speech, they deserve notice at this point.
- Definition: These are verb imposters. They smell, look, taste, feel, and sound like verbs, but they are not. There are three verbals: gerunds, infinitives, and participles.

- Gerund:

  o A gerund is always a noun that ends in –*ing*.

  o Example: <u>Walking</u> is great exercise. (*Walking* here is used as a noun. Walking in this sentence is an activity, an exercise. In this sentence is takes the place of the noun.) Now look at this sentence: I am <u>walking</u> home today by myself. (*Walking* is now a part of the verb phrase "am walking." It is now an action. You must be able to tell whether something is an activity or an action. An activity is a noun, a thing. An action is some kind of physical or phenomenal motion. I am using the word *phenomenal* in the sense of constituting or relating to a phenomenon, a fact or occurrence that can be observed.)

  o Example: <u>Playing </u>can teach many social skills to children. (*Playing* is a noun, an activity, a thing. It is the subject of this sentence.) Here is what it looks like as a verb: I <u>am playing</u> chess on my iPhone. (Now *playing* is the main verb in this verb phrase. The present progressive verb form, *am playing*, is an action, a physical or phenomenal movement.

  o Here is one to think about: I love <u>playing</u> the guitar. Is *playing* a verb or a gerund?

- Infinitive:

  o An infinitive is *to* + verb, any verb.

  o Example: I want <u>to go</u> to the store. (In this sentence, *to go* is not part of the verb. It is that simple. If the word *to* is attached to any verb, *it cannot be a verb*. Example: I am going <u>to buy</u> that pair of shoes. (*To buy* is not part of the verb. The question is what is the subject—*I*—doing or being in this sentence. *I* in this sentence is "am going." *I* is not "to buy." That does not even make sense. "I am going" is the subject and verb of this sentence, not "I to buy." *To buy* is the infinitive.

- Participle:

  o A participle can function as a modifier. It can end in *–ed* or *–ing*. But a participle will never act as a noun, and that is how you can tell the difference between a gerund ending in *–ing* and a participle ending in *–ing*.
  o Example: I am a <u>loving</u> man. (In this sentence *loving* is used as an adjective describing *man*.)
  o Example: She is a <u>wanted </u>woman. (Again, the participle, *wanted*, is describing *woman*.)

I am of the persuasion that verbals are not verb forms and definitely not verbs. But they do share a physical relationship to verbs. It is their appearance that connects them to verbs in our minds. They do not serve the function or fit the definition of verbs; therefore, verbals are not verbs but are verb imposters.

Conjunction:

- Definition: connecting words that have two functions—subordinate and coordinate.
- Function: links sentences, clauses, phrases, or words.
- **Subordinate conjunctions** connect independent clauses to dependent clauses or vice versa. There are several

subordinate conjunctions: *because, if, since, while, when, if, although, before, after,* and so forth. Each of these words places a condition on the clause that it is attached to, thus making the clause dependent on the condition being met.

o   Example: I love you <u>because</u> you have loved me unconditionally.

- **Coordinate conjunctions** connect equal parts: a word with a word, a phrase with a phrase, a clause with a clause, and a sentence with a sentence. A coordinate conjunction acts like a fulcrum; it provides balance for a sentence. There are only seven of these, and each has a particular meaning: *for* = because, *and* = in addition to, *nor* = negative choice, *but* = contrast, *or* = positive choice, *yet* = contrast, *so* = results. The acronym FANBOYS can help you remember this list of coordinating conjunctions.

o   Example: I am no longer able to see you, <u>nor</u> am I able to communicate with you. (*Nor* is connecting a sentence with a sentence. When *nor* is used, the subject and verb in the second clause usually switch places.)

Adverb:

- Definition: a word that modifies verbs, adjectives, and other adverbs.
- Functions: modifies a verb, an adjective, another adverb, or a sentence (e.g., *happily, very,* or *frankly*). Adverbs answer these questions: how, where, when, and to what degree.

- Proper usage: She ran <u>very</u> fast. He was <u>somewhat</u> happy. He <u>very quickly</u> turned to run. I am going <u>downtown</u> this <u>afternoon</u>.

Adjective:

- Definition: a word that describes nouns or pronouns.
- Function: describes or qualifies a noun or pronoun. Adjectives answer these questions: what kind, which one, and how many.
- Proper usage: Her love feels like a <u>warm</u> blanket on a <u>cold</u> night.
- Article (*A, an,* and *the* are adjectives that are called articles.)

  o Definition: noun indicator.
  o Function: points out person, places, and things.
  o Proper usage: <u>A</u> cowboy should not hurt <u>an </u>Indian because that would break <u>the </u>natural laws of ethics. (Use *a* before words that start with consonants and *an* before any words that start with or sound like they begin with a vowel. Example: <u>an</u> honor. *An* should be used here because honor sounds like it begins with an *o*.)

Preposition:

- Definition: (1) a word or group of words that shows the relationship between two things in time or space; (2) a word that connects the object of a sentence to the rest of the sentence.

- Function: (1) a word or group of words that illustrates the relationship of two things in time or space; (2) a word that connects an object (usually) to the pronoun or noun that came before it.
- Proper usage: (1) The tennis balls were <u>under</u> his bed. (2) My daughter handed her report card <u>to</u> me.

Interjection:

- Definition: an exclamation expressing emotions.
- Function: a sound, word, or phrase that expresses a strong emotion, such as pain or surprise but otherwise has no meaning.
- Proper usage: <u>Wow</u>, she is beautiful!

Learning grammar is important for being able to write properly in the English language. But learning grammar can be tricky at times because context changes meaning and usage. The best aid to studying grammar is to read fun and interesting material, paying special attention to the grammar (how the eight parts of speech are used). The complementary activity to pair with reading is writing in a daily journal while being present and aware of the definitions and functions of proper grammar. This is equivalent to providing yourself with an extra helping of writer's steroids (the legal stuff, of course). It does not matter in the beginning what you read or what you write about in your journal. As long as you are becoming more aware and skillful with the use of grammar, you are on track to becoming a better writer. You improve as a writer as you read increasingly challenging material, stuff that makes you think, feel, or examine deeply any content that goes beyond your personal perspective. Set out with the intention to gain a command of the usage of grammar and to develop the skill of writing clearly and effectively in English.

One of my students asked me, "Doesn't adhering to all these rules of grammar stifle the creative spirit?" I answered, "It doesn't have to. But for most students it does. It did for me. But now I feel like an artist having fun every time I write." That question did enough to rekindle my appreciation for writing. I realized that when I write I feel like I am creating a living being, a work of living art. But it was mastering the rules and guidelines of writing that permitted me this power. It was the hours of reading and writing thousands of pages that gave birth to the writer and teacher within. Even if you do not aspire to be a writer, you must know grammar in order to read and write at higher and higher levels. And in order to gain command of the written word, you must develop a willingness to put in the work that will awaken your writer's voice and the teacher within.

Works Cited

Barrett, Jeffrey Alan. *The Quantum Mechanics of Minds and Worlds.* Oxford: Oxford University Press, 1999.

Bohm, David. *Wholeness and the implicate order.* London: Routledge & Kegan Paul, 1980.

Bohm, David. "A New Theory of the Relationship of Mind and Matter." 1980. *Philosophical Psychology*: 271-286.

Bohr, Niels. *Atomic Theory and the Description of Nature (The Philosophical Writings of Niels Bohr, Vol. I).* Woodbridge, Conn.: Ox Bow Press, 1987.

Cabane, Olivia Fox. *The Charisma Myth: How Anyone Can Caster the Art and Science of Personal Magnetism.* New York: Portfolio/Penguin, 2012.

Inside Job. DVD. Directed by Charles H. Ferguson. Culver City, Calif.: Sony Pictures Home Entertainment, 2011.

Frankl, Viktor E. *Man's Search for Meaning.* Boston: Beacon Press, 2006.

Lee, Ilchi. *Brain Wave Vibration: Getting Back into the Rhythm of a Happy, Healthy Life.* Sedona, Ariz.: Best Life Media, 2008.

Moller, Aage R. *The Malleable Brain Benefits and Harm from Plasticity of the Brain.* New York: Nova Biomedical Books, 2009.

Rogers, Kara. *The Brain and the Nervous System.* New York, NY: Britannica Educational Pub., in association with Rosen Educational Services, 2011.

Schrodinger, Erwin. *What is life?: The Physical Aspect of the Living Cell; & Mind and Matter.* Cambridge: University Press, 1967.

Schucman, Helen. *A Course In Miracles text, workbook for students, manual for teachers.* Original ed. Tiburon, CA: Foundation for Inner Peace, 1976.

Bibliography

Lanza, R. P., and Bob Berman. *Biocentrism: How Life and Consciousness Are the Keys to Understanding the True Nature of the Universe.* Dallas, TX: BenBella Books, Inc., 2009.

Mulford, Prentice. *Thoughts Are Things: Essays Selected from the White Cross Library.* Santa Fe, NM: Sun Books, 1993.

Murphy, Joseph. *The Power of Your Subconscious Mind.* Englewood Cliffs, N.J.: Prentice-Hall, 1963.

Ruiz, Miguel. *The Four Agreements: A Practical Guide to Personal Freedom.* San Rafael, Calif.: Amber-Allen Pub., 1997.

Suzuki, Shunryu, and Trudy Dixon. *Zen Mind, Beginner's Mind.* 1st ed. New York: Walker/Weatherhill, 1970.

The Money Masters: How International Bankers Gained Control of America. DVD. Directed by Patrick S. J. Carmack and Bill Still. Manitou Springs, CO, 1996.

Vishton, Peter M. *Understanding the Secrets of Human Perception.* Chantilly, Va.: Teaching Company, 2011.

Zeitgeist Addendum. DVD. Directed by Peter Joseph. S.l.: s.n., 2008.